Intervention Techniques For Child/Youth Care Workers

by
Mark A. Krueger, Ph.D.

Child Welfare League of America
440 First Street, NW, Suite 310
Washington, DC 20001-8025

CHILD WELFARE LEAGUE OF AMERICA, INC.
440 First Street, NW, Suite 310
Washington, DC 20001-2085

CURRENT PRINTING (last digit)
10 9 8 7 6 5 4 3 2

Cover design by Suzanne Van de Boom

PRINTED IN THE UNITED STATES OF AMERICA

ISBN # 0-87868-260-0

PREFACE

The publishing of *Intervention Techniques for Child/Youth Care Workers* is another important milestone in the development of the body of knowledge in the child and youth care field. Dr. Krueger's first book, *Intervention Techniques for Child Care Workers*, was the first book written in the United States by a practicing direct line child care worker. This second edition of "Intervention Techniques" is a further refinement of the basic theories and concepts presented in the first book.

The tone and style of this book are similar to those in the first one. The tone is one of caring and advocacy for children. It is apparent that the author has been there. He has felt and experienced the things that he writes about. The style is clear and comfortable, and one which communicates to the direct service worker, the supervisior, and the administrator. Throughout the book there is a motif of support and conviction for children and youth.

This book has a definite theoretical position. However, the emphasis is consistently on the practical application of the theory. This is the appropriate emphasis for any book which attempts to provide youth and child care workers with behavior management and intervention strategies. Unlike other books published for workers in the field, this one provides the reader with very specific examples, directions and models.

Upon reviewing the table of contents, some might argue that these topics are not new and are similar to ones that have been written about before. There is certainly some truth to that position. However, I continue to be astonished as I travel throughout North America at how few workers, supervisiors, and administrators still, to this day, are aware of the established basic principles and concepts of working effectively with children. A frightening number of directors and clinicians in programs for children and youth have never heard of people like Fritz Redl, Albert Trieschman, Bruno Bettleheim, and their classical works and writings in this field. To those of us who are actively involved in this work and the establishment of the profession, it is a serious mistake to assume that many of the principles and theories that we feel represent the foundations of the field have been accepted by all those who are involved in daily practice and direct work. This is clearly not the case.

Thus, it is quite appropriate that this and other books like *Intervention Techniques for Child/Youth Care Workers* continue to be written until there is widespread awareness and the emergence of some theoretical bases of knowledge in the practice of youth and child care work.

It has been said that "truth for an individual exists only to the extent to which he or she is willing to put it into action." Throughout his professional life Mark Krueger has put his beliefs and convictions about youth and child care practice into action. This recent publication of *Intervention Techniques for Child/Youth Care Workers* is another manifestation of Dr. Krueger's commitment to the practice, involvement, and constructive action.

Norman W. Powell, Jr.
*President, National Organization of
    Child Care Worker Associations.*

INTRODUCTION

Child/youth care workers who work with troubled youths in residential treatment centers, group homes, temporary shelter care facilities, correctional facilities, and home and community service programs are in a unique treatment position. Unlike other helping adults in these programs, their interactions with youths usually span the total day. This allows them to seize numerous treatment opportunities which are not available to less involved professionals. For example, child/youth care workers are generally on hand to encourage youths to learn when they are most motivated, to reward change as it occurs, and to discuss feelings when youths are ready. These are advantages that can ensue only from extensive involvement with troubled youths.

This book is designed to assist workers in their efforts to maximize, intensify or simply "get the most" from their daily interactions with troubled youths by offering dozens of techniques and programs which workers can choose from to add to their repertoire of child/youth caring skills. All of the techniques and programs are based on my experiences as a child/youth care worker. These firsthand accounts of direct-line practice should make the book useful and practical for experienced and inexperienced workers. The book, however, is not intended to be substituted as a handbook for child/youth care work. Instead, it is recommended as a training or self instruction manual that can be used to augment the reader's understanding of child/youth care work with specific how-to practices and methods of procedure.

This work is a major revision of the original Intervention Techniques for Child Care Workers which is currently being used by workers and instructors across the United States and Canada. In this edition, the content has been altered to reach a broader audience, several new techniques have been added and emphasis has been placed on training and self instruction; however, I have also tried to maintain the original flavor which emanated from being the first book written by a practicing child/youth care worker.

A systematic or "big picture to small picture" learning approach is the foundation for content presentation. The objectives are to first show how general intervention concepts are interrelated and to then move on to explain specific intervention techniques and programs. For example, chapters and major topic sections are organized to present concepts central to understanding why and how intervention techniques are used before presenting instructions for using specific techniques. This approach was chosen because the current state of the child/youth care art is based on systematic intervention. In other words, effective child/youth care workers do not haphazardly intervene with troubled youth. Their interventions are based on a certain philosophy or plan which represents the consensus of a team of workers working with a specific group of youths and which is consistent with the realities of their treatment environment.

Chapter One, "Intervention Prerequisites," provides essential information for understanding and using the techniques and programs in the following chapters. The prerequisites include: a relevant perspective for understanding troubled youths and their behavior, a definition of intervention techniques, characteristics for effective treatment environments and three assessment areas for using intervention techniques.

Chapter Two, "Observing and Reporting Techniques," Chapter Three, "Group Activity Techniques," Chapter Four, "Reinforcement Techniques," and Chapter Five, "Discipline Alternatives to Punishment," include specific intervention techniques. Each chapter begins with a generic definition of the techniques presented in the chapter. Techniques are then sequentially presented under major topic headings. For example, under the topic heading, "18. Privilege Systems," seven, techniques numbered one through seven are presented with instructions for using each technique. The book has a total of one hundred twelve techniques.

Chapter Six, "Self Care Programs," and Chapter Seven, "Social Interaction Programs," include examples of treatment programs or systematic approaches to treating major developmental strengths and weaknesses. The objective here is to show how the intervention techniques presented in previous chapters and new techniques can be integrated into comprehensive programs. All thirteen of the programs in these chapters were designed and implemented by teams of child/youth care workers.

Readers will receive the most benefit from this experience if three general rules or principles are kept in mind while reading through the chapters. First, it is important to get a good grasp of the concepts presented in Chapter One, at the beginning of each chapter and under each major topic heading before attempting to learn how to use specific techniques. All of the techniques have an interrelated purpose and, therefore, it is not realistic to expect a technique to be effective without a broader understanding of various related issues. Second, techniques may have to be adapted to meet specific needs. This process can be facilitated by discussions with fellow team members or supervisors. Third, there are no quick-fix solutions in this book. All of the techniques take time and patience to master.

A further caution or reminder is to be aware that techniques are only as good as the relationships which exist among adults and youths in a treatment environment. In a recent interview, Dr. Albert Trieschman, a prominent leader in the field, commented: "Child care workers must be careful not to let their techniques get between them and the children." The message here is that workers should not use techniques to do something *to* youths. Techniques are used *with* youths at a pace which is consistent with developing relationships.[1]

Troubled youths are defined as emotionally disturbed, dependent and neglected and/or delinquent youths ages 6-17. Child/youth care workers are the adults who spend considerable time interacting with and treating troubled youths in the daily living environment of youth care programs. The daily living environment usually encompasses all of the places and hours in a day when youths are not in a traditional school or therapy setting. However, in recent years, workers have also been spending more time providing services which were formerly handled or delivered only by teachers and social workers. For example, it is not unusual for a child/youth care worker to be designated by a treatment team as the primary therapist or instructor of special subjects for a specific youth.

The terms "child/youth care worker" and "troubled youths" have been chosen as opposed to the more traditional "child care worker" and "troubled" or "emotionally disturbed children" to avoid confusion with child care workers working with younger children in a variety of day care and day treatment settings. This terminology also seems to be consistent with the direction chosen by the child care profession in its attempts to clarify the roles and titles of its members. The intent, however, is not to minimize the many similarities that exist in the needs of older and younger children and the roles of the child or youth care workers in all sectors of the human service system. There are, indeed, many more similarities than differences.

While many of the techniques reflect my experiences and the experiences of my child/youth care peers working in residential treatment centers, alterations have been made to accommodate the needs of workers in more and less restrictive environments, and in longer and shorter term programs. Many of the techniques are also relevant for an increasing number of workers who are working with troubled youths and their families in their own homes.

1. Quote taken from the video tape series entitled *The Anger Within*. Silver Spring, Maryland: NAK Productions, 1981.

CONTENTS

CHAPTER ONE

INTERVENTION PREREQUISITES

The first chapter is designed to provide a foundation or the "big picture" for the book. In this context, each section of the chapter is considered to be an essential prerequisite for the intervention techniques and programs that follow. Hence, readers are encouraged to become familiar with the concepts presented here before moving on to the next chapter.

The major concepts in the chapter include, in order, (a) a perspective for understanding troubled youths and their behavior, (b) a definition of intervention techniques, (c) essential characteristics for effective intervention environments, and (d) general assessment areas for using intervention techniques.

Understanding Troubled Youths and Their Behavior

The perspective for understanding troubled youths and their behavior presented in this section is intended to augment, not replace, the readers' existing knowledge of troubled youths. It includes relevant concepts which underlie the selection of techniques and programs offered later. Most readers will be able to integrate this information into their own conceptual framework for intervention. If this is a first exposure to troubled youths, additional readings will be needed to obtain a broader understanding of issues. There are several excellent references in the list of suggested readings at the end of this book.

Presenting Problems

Troubled youths generally have not experienced the same quality and quantity of care and learning in their relationships with adults and peers as other youths their age and this makes it difficult for them to feel worthwhile and to function as productive members of our society. More specifically, without fulfilling relationships, troubled youths are not able to develop the skills, feelings and thought processes that will allow them to develop the way other youths do. Following are descriptions of how relationships can affect troubled youths in three major areas of development.

Emotional Development

Troubled youths' emotional involvement with others has usually been permeated by impermanence and unpredictability. They have been abandoned frequently, both psychologically and physically, and they have been exposed to an inordinate amount of extreme emotional behavior. This creates at least three major problems. First, they experience an excess of depression, guilt, anger, fear, rejection and loss. And, when these are their prevailing emotions, it is difficult for them to feel good about themselves and their environment. Second, they do not learn how to cope with and express their feelings. They will often cover-up, misdirect or act out rather than share their feelings in a more self-fulfilling way. Finally, troubled youths will often behave as if they don't care about how others feel. They will ignore or belittle others instead of trying to be helpful or compassionate. All of these factors serve to constantly deprive troubled youths of the relationships and interactions they need to develop the emotional strengths required to deal with the stress, anxiety and enjoyment of everyday living.

Cognitive Development

Troubled youths have also related to adults and peers who have been unable to provide the cognitive stimulation and insight they need to cope successfully with the realities of their immediate living environment. Generally they have a distorted knowledge of the world around them, a limited awareness of how to interact socially with others and inadequate problem solving techniques. For instance, their world view may be completely inconsistent with realilty. What seems obvious and logical to them may be in complete opposition to what others around them perceive as obvious or logical. Troubled youths also have trouble "placing themselves in another person's shoes." They are unaware that others have thoughts and feelings which are different from their thoughts and feelings. Hence, they often appear as if they are manipulating or twisting situations to meet their own needs at the expense of others.

Their reasoning processes also often leave them with the least rather than the most productive alternative. Even when more productive alternatives are readily available, they will pick the solution which can only lead to more problems. It is almost as if they are driven to pick the wrong course in order to justify the poor images they have of themselves.[1]

Physical Development

Another frequent outcome of troubled youths'

relationships is physical neglect. They are often underweight or overweight, afflicted with minor illnesses or suffering from lack of proper nutrition. Their coordination, balance, manual dexterity and other basic movements are also often awkward or underdeveloped in comparison to other youths their age. Troubled youths also often have a neglected looking or disheveled physical appearance.

Problems in these three areas of development are compounded further by the fact that each area can have an effect on the other two areas. Lack of emotional, cognitive and physical growth are usually mutually interdependent. Problems in one area enhance the probability of problems in another area. Just as one's positive strengths can build upon each other, negative traits can perpetuate each other. It is not surprising, then, that troubled youths develop feelings and perceptions about themselves, others and the world they live in which make it difficult for them to get involved in growing experiences such as daily living routines, recreational activities, school, and positive interactions with adults and peers. For example, some troubled youths are so used to not having their emotional, cognitive and physical needs met that, to them, growing up just means more unmet needs. Other youths have such poor self images and feelings of self worth that they can't imagine themselves as being eligible for positive change.

Still other youths are afraid to try something new, because they think others expect more than they can give. And even when their perceptions of others' expectations are fairly accurate, their perceptions of their own abilities might not be sufficient to allow them to try.

Finally, troubled youths often are not able to identify a place for themselves in the world. No one in the past seemed to care enough to show them where they fit in and they can't define their own place, so as far as they are concerned they really do not belong here.

Circular Effect Behavior Patterns

Troubled youths' perception and feelings are often manifest in behavior patterns which create circular effects. A circular effect occurs when a person behaves negatively and others in turn are forced to respond negatively. For example, a youth begins to hit other youths and the adult responds by isolating the youth in a confinement room, which makes the youth continue to feel worthless. These situations create growth stalemates, because nothing transpires to improve the youths' feelings and perceptions about themselves, others and the world they live in.

Behavior patterns which create circular effects are often called defense or avoidance mechanisms. These patterns are also identified by specific terms such as manipulation, scapegoating, hyperactivity, aggressive behavior, passive behavior, temper tantrums, acting out and running away (additional circular effect behavior patterns are listed in Table 1.)

TABLE 1
CIRCULAR EFFECT BEHAVIOR PATTERNS

Poor grooming habits

Poor eating habits

Scapegoating

Preoccupation with issues other than those at hand

Covering up or going through the motions without really trying

Manipulating others

Not following through with responsibilities to others

Antagonizing others with verbal abuse

Temper tantrums

Fighting

Running away

Breaking rules: of the game
                        of the program
                        of the group
                        of society

Destroying property

Invading others' privacy

Not communicating

Circular effect behavior patterns usually lead to interrupted growing experiences because: (a) adults are forced to use punitive solutions which emphasize removal instead of involvement, (b) the behavior is so disruptive that the ongoing activity must be

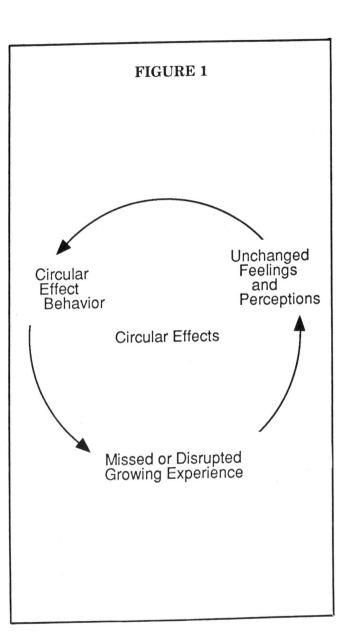

FIGURE 1

Circular
Effect
Behavior

Unchanged
Feelings
and
Perceptions

Circular Effects

Missed or Disrupted
Growing Experience

discontinued, or (c) youths disguise their involvement by merely going through the motions with very little self investment. Any one of these situations alone can eliminate a growing experience and create a growth stalemate for the youth. And when circular effect behavior patterns are the primary means of interaction, as is often the case within groups of troubled youths, it is extremely difficult for the adult to create an environment in which some form of growth can take place.

Readers can no doubt add additional circular effect behavior patterns and identify more reasons or causes for the behavior. In each case it will be apparent that, unless self-defeating circular effects are broken, the youth will continue to remain troubled.

Figure 1 depicts a typical circular effect. The youth displays a circular effect behavior pattern leading to an interrupted or missed growing experience and consequently, the youth's perceptions and feelings about himself, others and the world he lives in remain unchanged or become even more distorted or negative.

Intervention Techniques

Intervention techniques are the practices or methods of procedure child/youth care workers use to break through circular effects. The generic terms for the techniques presented in this book are: *observing* and *reporting techniques, group activity techniques, reinforcement techniques* and *discipline techniques*. When these techniques are used individually or in combination, workers can place themselve in a position where they can promote feelings of self worth, positive relationships and new learning, rather than having to constantly react with punitive or growth stalemating alternatives.

Intervention techniques can also be used to promote troubled youths' many strengths. Positive behaviors were not discussed in the previous section, but readers should be aware that troubled youths have the ability to exhibit behavior patterns which create positive circular effects. These behaviors will be highlighted throughout the book.

Intervention techniques generally have three major purposes: prevention, support and correction. The **preventive purpose** is to create an environment in which the probability that youths will develop productive alternatives is increased, and the probability that they will continue to create negative circular effects decreased. The **supportive purpose** is to provide immediate encouragement and reinforcement for changing feelings, thoughts and behaviors, and for continued efforts to build upon strengths. And, the **corrective purpose** is to provide a logical, nonpunitive consequence for an inappropriate behavior pattern.

Any one technique may fulfill one, two or three of the intervention purposes. However, most techniques have a primary purpose. Techniques with a primary prevention purpose are **indirect techniques**. These techniques are usually employed before a child/youth care worker interacts with youth. For example, observing, reporting and activity planning techniques are preventive techniques which workers use to increase the effectiveness of later interactions

FIGURE 2

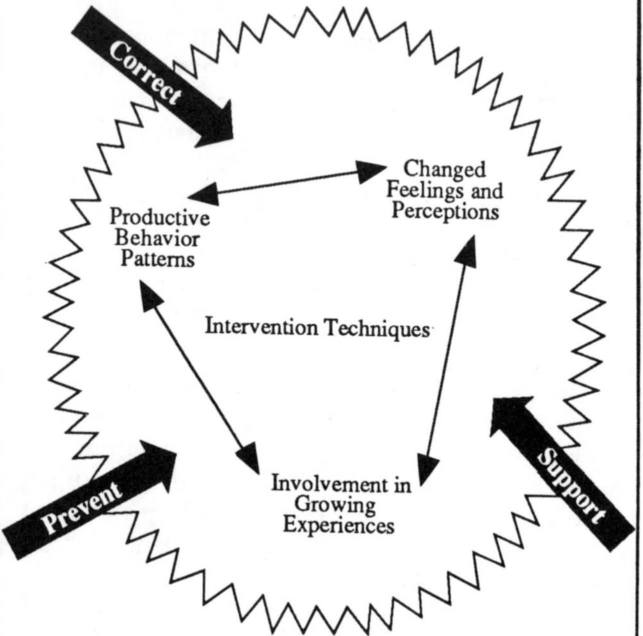

Correct

Prevent

Support

Changed Feelings and Perceptions

Productive Behavior Patterns

Intervention Techniques

Involvement in Growing Experiences

with the youth. Techniques with primary supportive and corrective purpose are **direct techniques**. These techniques are used while the workers are interacting with youth. For example, praise and time outs are supportive and corrective techniques respectively which workers use to improve the quality of ongoing interactions with youth.

The purposes for the intervention techniques will be identified at the beginning of each technique chapter. Techniques will generally be presented in the order established above; prevention, support, and correction. This order has been chosen because intervention techniques are more effective if child/youth care workers think prevention first and correction last. When correction is first in the minds of child/youth care workers, most of their time is spent dealing with inappropriate behavior after it has occurred and this is the least productive way to intervene.

The intervention process is depicted in Figure 2. Child/youth care workers break through circular effects by intervening with preventive, supportive and corrective techniques. The point at which they intervene and how they intervene is dependent upon the youth's specific needs and presenting problems. These interventions, in turn, lead to more productive behavior patterns, involvement in growing experiences, and changed perceptions and feelings.

Ingredients for Effective
Intervention Environment

There are several key program ingredients which are essential prerequisites for using intervention techniques. In other words, child/youth care workers attempting to use intervention techniques will have a much greater chance of success if they work in youth care programs with similar ingredients to the ones listed below. This does not mean that programs will not have shortcomings or be missing one or more of these ingredients, but it does mean that administrators and staff must be constantly working toward blending similar ingredients into program philosophy and actions.

Commitment to Caring Relationships

Caring relationships are the most important ingredient in any program for troubled youths. The "core of care," however, takes time to develop.[2] The trust, attachment, empathy, compassion and security which comprise the core cannot be developed through passing encounters with a number of child/youth care workers. Caring relationships require a commitment to and from workers. Consequently, in effective programs, administrators express a strong commitment to the caring role of the worker and support their commitment with incentives, training and supervision for the workers. The workers respond by making a commitment to remain with the organization and by using available resources to continually upgrade their interactions with the youth.

Developmental Dynamics

The bulk of treatment for troubled youths will take place in daily interactions among the youths and the child/youth care workers. When the environment is planned and structured to emphasize daily interactions which enhance emotional, cognitive and physical growth, there is no more potent force for helping troubled youths. When programs ignore or downplay this crucial aspect of treatment, the youths are shortchanged. Effective programs have mechanisms for assessing youths' current levels of development and encourage the use of intervention strategies which begin by meeting needs at assessed levels of development and proceed by building upon existing strengths and by developing new strengths.

Planned Daily Activities

Planned involvement in self care, academic, vocational, and recreational activities is part of the central focus of successful programs. Troubled youths need extensive involvement with peers and adults in activities which promote mastery of daily living skills, develop academic and vocational skills, and enhance artistic, musical and athletic abilities. These are the activities that most program managers believe will help troubled youth to be independent, to problem solve, and to create their own fun and enjoyment. However, program managers will also agree that these activities can be easily lost in the shuffle of daily interactions or be interrupted by circular effect behavior. Therefore, successful programs emphasize advance planning to eliminate as much confusion and disruption as possible.

Family involvement

Youths need continual involvement with their families, even youths who come from very disruptive families. This involvement, however, should not be limited to traditional family therapy. Family members want to know how to manage, teach, parent, and enjoy their youths, and most troubled youths need continuous interaction with their parents and siblings. Therefore, effective programs involve families in as many child/youth care facets of the program as are reasonably possible.

Discipline Alternatives to Punishment

Troubled youths do not need more punishment. If punishment were the answer, most of them would be exemplary citizens. They have been punished throughout their lives, many of them physically punished, and even more of them pyschologically punished. Hence, effective programs try to expose youths to the many discipline alternatives to punishment which have been developed over the past years. For example, there are discipline techniques which emphasize self discipline or internal control as an alternative to external punishment imposed by adults (Chapter Five). These alternatives have a much better prognosis for success, but also require time, patience, and commitment to deliver.

Team Decision-Making

Child/youth care workers are rarely the sole implementers of an intervention technique. They are usually part of a team of workers who are responsible for choosing and implementing intervention techniques for a specific group of children. Teams can be as large as ten members and as small as two members. Some teams have members from several departments in addition to the child/youth care department and other teams have members from only one or two departments. No matter how small or large the team, the objective is to reach consensus about how to intervene with each youth in the team's care. Agreements are obtained by a majority vote but members of the minority must also be willing to compromise in order to effectively implement team decisions. One or two members cannot be resisting or "doing their own thing" or the technique will fail.

Creating a consensus decision-making environment is not easy but it can be acomplished. Programs with effective consensus team decision-making usually have the following characteristics: (a) there is a strong commitment among administrators to promote professional equality for all team members; (b) in-service training emphasizes teamwork, communication, and reporting and observing skills; (c) working conditions and incentives are comparable for most team members; and (d) all team members have an opportunity to attend team decision-making meetings.[3]

Three Assessment Areas: The Treatment Plan, Relationships and the Environment

Whenever possible, intervention techniques should be discussed and evaluated by the team before being used. It is difficult, if not impossible, to effectively employ intervention techniques without input from fellow team members and the knowledge that each technique serves the best interests of the youths and adults in the program. Child/youth care workers who must attempt to use intervention techniques in isolation from others and/or with haphazard selection processes are in an extremely detrimental position.

In this section, three assessment areas for using intervention techniques will be identified. These areas, along with specific information presented with each technique, are designed to help child/youth care workers determine whether or not an intervention technique is appropriate in their situation.

The Individual Treatment Plan

Most programs for troubled youths are required to have some type of individual treatment plan for each youth in the program. Treatment plans set the stage for all interactions with a specific youth. A well-constructed plan begins with the observations and recommendations of all the adults working with a specific youth and proceeds by setting intervention parameters which represent the consensus views of the adults about what has happened to the youth and what can be expected in the present and in the future.

When an intervention technique is being considered for use by an individual or team of workers, it should be discussed in relationship to the parameters specified in the treatment plan. The parameters usually include an assessment or diagnosis of the youth's various levels of emotional, cognitive, and physical development. The objective, then, is to select techniques which are appropriate for the assessed levels of development. For example, if the plan indicated a youth had poor hand-eye coordination, the team would not decide to expose the youth to hours of batting practice, nor would they leave a socially and emotionally dependent youth unsupervised for lengthy periods of time. Instead, the team might choose lead-up games which develop hand-eye coordination at a very basic level for the one youth, and planned group and individual interactions which lead to greater emotional and social independence for the other youth.

The decision about whether or not an intervention technique falls within treatment plan parameters has to be a joint decision among the adults who designed the plan. If the team decides the technique is appropriate, then it becomes an additional part of the plan. Intervention techniques are often included in the section of the plan called behavior change strategies or treatments. Then, once a technique becomes part of the plan, all the adults must try to be as consistent as possible in fulfilling their roles in implementing the technique. Thus, the treatment plan provides the first and perhaps most important assessment area for using intervention techniques. (Treatment Plans will also be discussed in Chapter Two.)

Relationships

Child/youth care workers have many different kinds of relationships with troubled youths. There are some youths they like very much, some they find hard to like and still others they don't know how to feel about. Youths in turn also have mixed feelings about their workers. There are some they get very attached to, others they do not get close to and still others they are apprehensive and uncertain about. Relationships are also in a constant state of development. Workers and youths are always at different points of involvement in the program. Some workers have been with the youths for several months and others just a few days. And the youths can be in a beginning, middle or final stage of treatment. Thus, no two relationships have the same significance, nor the same stage of development.

When teams of workers are in the process of deciding whether or not to use a technique, it is important to assess the significance of the various relationships team members have with the youth. A technique could be very effective for one worker with a specific kind of relationship and toally ineffective for a worker with another kind of relationship. The objectives are to determine how relationships can or cannot be used in implementing a technique. For example, the team may want to use a reinforcement technique which requires a trusting relationship to implement. If only one or two team members have this trusting relationship, the team may decide to allow to let just the two workers use the technique and/or search for a technique which more members can use.

Team members can determine the significance of their relationships with the youths by offering each other constructive criticism, positive feedback and objective insights which will help assess the specific nature of individual relationships. It is not always easy to communicate this information to fellow team members, especially when one worker is struggling or having a difficult time developing relationships, but if workers aren't willing to be open, honest and direct with each other, they will often be using techniques which are not appropriate for their relationships with the youth. It is difficult, if not impossible, to assess the significance of one's relationships with youths without help from fellow workers.

The Intervention Environment

Treatment programs have complex intervention environments. The place in which an intervention is to occur, the people using the technique and the time of day for intervening are just a few of the factors that can come into play with a specific intervention technique. These factors must always be given consideration or a technique can easily be out of synch with its environment. For example, child/youth care workers who attempt to reward a youth for appropriate touching at night on the playground where they cannot accurately observe how the youth is touching will obviously not have an opportunity to effectively employ the reward technique. Or, if a team is attempting to use a behavior management technique for hitting which requires immediate follow through, and several team members are unable to follow through immediately, the technique will lose its impact.

Usually techniques are adapted to the environment. For example, a game of four square may be played instead of basketball if the basketball court is not available. But environments can also be altered to accommodate more effective techniques. For example, the place in which meals are eaten or the number of youths eating at any given time may be changed to provide an atmosphere more conducive to quiet mealtime discussion. Whichever course is chosen, adaption or accommodation, the environment should always be recognized as playing a key role in the intervention process.

The assessment process is outlined in Figure 3. First, a problem or strength is identified and formally or informally agreed upon by a team of workers. Second, one or more members of the team proposes an intervention strategy or technique. Third, team members assess the technique according to the treatment plan, their relationships with the youth, and the realities of their intervention environment. Finally, if the technique is acceptable, it is integrated into the treatment plan and remains a part of the plan until a review or further assessments indicate it is no longer needed.

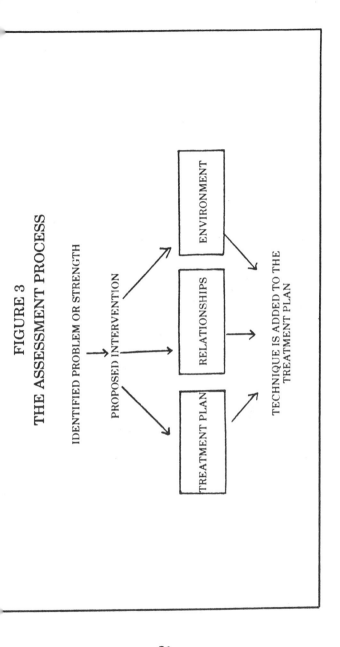

FIGURE 3
THE ASSESSMENT PROCESS

IDENTIFIED PROBLEM OR STRENGTH

PROPOSED INTERVENTION

ENVIRONMENT

RELATIONSHIPS

TREATMENT PLAN

TECHNIQUE IS ADDED TO THE
TREATMENT PLAN

21

Summary

The groundwork for intervention techniques has been laid in this chapter. The perspective for understanding troubled youth and their behavior, the definition of intervention techniques, the ingredients for effective intervention techniques and the three assessment areas for using intervention techniques will underlie all further presentations of intervention techniques. It is important, therefore, that the readers not move on unless a good grasp of these basic concepts has been obtained. Furthermore, readers should by now have begun to explore various ways in which these concepts can be adapted to their specific needs.

1. Lerner, R. *Concepts and theories of human development.* Reading, Mass: Addison-Wesley, 1976.

2. Maier, H. The core of care: essential ingredients for the development of children away from home. *Child Care Quarterly*, 1979, 8, (3) 161-173.

3. Krueger, M. *Implementation of a team decision-making model ,among child care workers.* Doctoral Dissertation, University of Wisconsin-Milwaukee, 1982.

CHAPTER TWO

OBSERVING AND REPORTING TECHNIQUES

Observing and reporting techniques are the procedures child/youth care workers use to record and share their daily observations with fellow team members during the treatment planning process. Since workers generally spend the most time interacting with and observing youths, the course of each youth's treatment is dependent on how well workers use these techniques to share their observations. When their observations are clearly articulated and integrated into the planning process, the effectiveness of future interventions can be significantly increased. On the other hand, without a sufficient effort to share these observations, the final treatment plan may lack the intensity and accuracy that can only come from the worker's firsthand impressions and interpretations.

Workers are counted on to share their observations in three stages of the treatment planning process: the intake stage, the middle or intermediate stage, and the discharge stage. The intake stage includes the decision to accept the youth into the program and the youth's initial adjustment to the program. The middle or intermediate stage focuses on developing relationships and strengths needed to move toward discharge and the discharge stage includes the decision to phase the youth out of the program and follow-up treatment strategies.

In each stage of the planning process, child/youth care workers report relevant observations and make recommendations for future change at a variety of formal and informal meetings. This information is used by the team to make assessments or diagnostic evaluations to develop treatment strategies and to evaluate progress. For example, information presented by workers is used to pinpoint emotional, cognitive and physical development problems, to design intervention techniques and to evaluate progress toward individual goals and objectives.

The techniques presented in this chapter are preventive techniques designed to help child/youth care workers become active participants in the treatment planning process at their agencies. Each technique serves the ultimate purpose of improving the quality of interactions with youth through development of effective treatment plans. The techniques include:

1. Observational Questioning
2. Log Note Writing
3. Charting
4. Report Writing
5. Recommending
6. Summarizing

While most of the discussion in this chapter focuses on the treatment planning process, alert readers will notice that observing and reporting techniques will also help them prepare other contributions such as articles, books and workshops. In other words, readers who are interested in making professional contributions to the child/youth care knowledge base will be able to use these same techniques to help draw forth accurate information about their child/youth care experiences.

1. Observational Questioning Techniques

Observational questioning is a process which helps child/youth care workers step back and reflect upon daily interactions with youths. When used properly, observational questioning allows the worker to objectively define, quantify and sort out relevant observations about interactions. It also improves the worker's ability to make meaningful personal interpretations of observations.

The objectives are to develop a list of questions about as many facets of youths' involvement in the program as possible and to seek logical explanations for answers to the questions. This information can then be shared with fellow workers through various forms of reporting such as planning meetings, log notes, recommendations, written reports and informal discussions. Following are six observational questioning techniques:

1.1 **Use existing treatment plans and social histories (if available), fellow workers, and your knowledge of troubled youths in general to identify ten or more major observation categories.** These categories should cover the major areas of intervention in your program. For example, categories might be entitled: Daily Living Habits, Personal Appearance, Health, Motor Abilities, Cognitive Abilities, Inappropriate Behavior Patterns, Appropriate Behavior Patterns,

Preventive and Supportive Techniques, Corrective Techniques and Personal Observations.

1.2 **Develop a list of specific questions for each category by once again using the above references.** Be as specific as possible and include as many questions as are appropriate at a given point in time. The list will expand and contract according to the needs of the program and individual youth in the program. Following is a list of the questions I used while working as a child/youth care workers:

Daily Living Habits

1. Does the Youth have a large, average or small appetite?
2. Is he sloppy or overly concerned about his manners at the dinner table?
3. Does he have regular or irregular toilet habits? Does he wet or soil? If he does, in my opinion, is the reason physical, emotional, lack of training, or some combination of the three?
4. What kind of sleeping habits does the youth have?
5. Can he perform normal grooming tasks? Does he know how to shower, wash up, comb his hair, brush his teeth and clip his fingernails?
6. Does he take care of his possessions? Can he make his bed and hang up his clothes? Does he keep track of his toys and put them away when he is finished

using them? Is he careless with his possessions? If he is, in what way, i.e., does he give them away, destroy them, or constantly lose them?

Physical Appearance

1. Does his height and weight compare to normal ranges for his age?
2. Are there any physical characteristics that appear abnormal?
3. Does he generally appear happy, enthused, responsive or depressed and despondent?
4. What are my impressions of his overall appearance?

Health

1. Does the youth suffer from an abnormal amount of minor illnesses?
2. Are there signs of seizures not previously reported?
3. Any major illness?
4. Are there any allergies or sight and hearing problems not reported previously?
5. How are the youth's teeth and general dental condition?
6. Are any of the youth's health problems related to psychological factors, poor eating habits, poor self-care habits or do illnesses seem primarily related to normal causes?

Motor Abilities

1. Is the youth's coordination good, average or poor?
2. If there is a gross motor or perceptual motor difficulty, how is it manifested? For example, does the youth have a problem holding a fork? Can he catch a ball thrown from a distance? Can he run, skip, hop? Does he have difficulty judging the closeness of objects to his body? Is he generally clumsy?
3. Is professional testing needed for assessing potential gross or perceptual motor difficulties?

Cognitive Abilities

1. In my opinion, is the youth's level of intelligence high, average or low?
2. Are his perceptions of the environment around him generally adequate or inadequate?
3. Are his perceptions or insights about others generally adequate or inadequate?
4. Are his communication skills good, average or poor?
5. Is his thinking capacity logical? Does he distort reality? Is he capable of hypothetical deductive reasoning or are his thoughts primarily concrete and object related?

Inappropriate Social Behaviors

1. Does the child avoid group involvement? Is he manipulative, physically aggressive, infantile or possessive? Does he cry, run away, lie, steal, swear or provoke others? Does he have temper tantrums?
2. How does this behavior affect the other group members?
3. How does the youth respond to adults? Does he resist, ignore, deny or respond in other negative ways?
4. How does his behavior towards me make me feel?
5. In my opinion, what is the youth trying to accomplish with his inappropriate social behavior? What causes him to behave this way?

Appropriate Social Behaviors

1. What behaviors make the youth likable? Is he friendly, intelligent, creative, sensitive to others or generally cheerful?
2. Does he follow routines and respond to adult instructions?
3. Does he participate in group activites?
4. Is he a positive leader or good model for other group members?
5. Is he affectionate and eager to please others?

Preventive and Supportive Techniques

1. What type of motivation seems to work best? Does he respond to praise and encouragement or is he more likely to respond to a material reward?
2. What activities does the youth enjoy and benefit from the most?
3. Are there specific problems that interfere more than others that could use special programming?
4. What cues indicate that the youth is about to act appropriately? How can the adult intervene when he sees these cues?

Managerial Techniques

1. How well does the youth respond to verbal instructions?
2. Can he follow more than one instruction at a time?
3. Is isolation from the group effective or ineffective?
4. If needed, how does the child respond to physical controls?
5. What consequences appear to be the most effective?
6. What techniques should be avoided?

Personal Observation

1. How do I feel about the youth and why?
2. How do I perceive the youth to feel about me and why?

1.3 **Read through the list until the questions in the list are very familiar.** Once you become accustomed to the questions, the list will be far less cumbersome than you may have originally anticipated.

1.4 **Select periods during the day to step back and review relevant questions and answers for each youth in the group.** Breaks and planning periods are good times to review questions. If these times are not available, then try to "think on your feet" whenever there is a break in the action.

1.5 **At the end of each shift, make a thorough examination of all pertinent questions and try to interpret the answers.** This is not nearly as difficult a process as it may seem. Questions which are most pertinent to a given youth's treatment will tend to stand out and those questions which are less meaningful will be easily skimmed over. After a short period of time you will be able to make descriptive statements such as "John combed his hair for the first time," "Mary played a game of checkers with Alice, the girl she was fighting with yesterday," "Pete did not respond to my verbal deescalation technique during his temper tantrum," "Sue ate everything on her plate tonight; this is the third day in a row she was able to eat a full meal," and "Bill approached me with a handshake instead of hitting me on the shoulder, three times today. I praised him after each occurence."

And you will be able to support these statements with further interpretations such as "I feel this may be a turning point in their relationship," "Based on my past three experiences with this verbal deescalation technique I do not feel this is an appropriate technique to use with his temper tantrums," and "Sue's increased appetite may be an indication that she is beginning to adjust to the program".

1.6 **Share descriptive statements and interpretations through the various reporting systems.** Several of these systems will be discussed in the following sections.

2. Log Note Techniques

Log notes are used mainly to communicate information from one team member to another. Each log indicates how well a specific youth has responded to the strategies outlined in the treatment plan and any new or unusual occurrences during the period of time in which the log note writer worked with a youth on any given day. The log reader uses this information to plan further interactions and/or to follow through with assignments from the writer.

Logs also provide data for more lengthy written reports and evaluations. For example, team members review their own and each other's logs when they are preparing consultation reports or filling out six-month evaluations.

Effective log use is dependent upon the writer and the reader having a good awareness of individual treatment plans. Logs are intended to be expedient, not lengthy narratives. Hence, log readers need a good awareness of intricacies related to each youth's treatment in order to get the most from the logs. Without a good awareness of specific treatment details, logs become exercises in futility, rather than an effective vehicle for communicating information and gathering data.

Following are two log note techniques:

2.1 **Use the observational questioning technique to draw out relevant information for the log.** While you are reviewing the list of questions, either make mental notes or jot down important information to be reported in the log. Then organize and summarize your thoughts according to the log note steps outlined below or develop a similar set of steps which are more related to your environment.

2.2 **Logs can be constructed in the following order:**
   a) Begin each log with a statement about how the youth responded to treatment on a given day or during a given period of time, i.e., "John had an unusually difficult day," or "Mary had an average

day."

b) Qualify statements with specific information to substantiate assessments, i.e., "I had to isolate him from the group on three occasions for starting fights," or "She continued to respond well to the reward program and she was an active participant in group discussions."

c) Offer an interpretation based on personal feelings and perceptions about the day's events, i.e., "I have a feeling John is very anxious about his upcoming home visit," or "It appears as if Mary is adjusting to the program and the group."

d) Offer alternative strategies and/or statements about unusual or encouraging events, i.e., "Afterwards I realized that I may have reduced his anxiety, at least enough to allow him to remain with the group, by selecting less stimulating activities," "John continues to do well on his grooming program and he seems to be complaining less about little aches and pains," or "Mary really likes getting her rewards. I also noticed by her body language that she is much more at ease during group discussions."

e) Add any information which is pertinent to the reader's duties during the next shift. i.e., "Don't forget his dentist appointment at 2:00," or "Please give

Mary ten bonus points for bedtime when she wakes up in the morning."

The two logs read as follows:

Ex. 1   John had an unusually difficult day. I had to isolate him from the group on three occasions for starting fights. I have a feeling John is very anxious about his upcoming home visit. Afterwards I realized that I may have reduced his anxiety, at least enough to allow him to remain with the group, by selecting less stimulating group activities. John continues to do well on his grooming program and he seems to be complaining less about little aches and pains. Don't forget his dentist appointment at 2:00.

Ex. 2   Mary had an average day. She continued to respond well to the reward program and she was an active participant in group discussions. It appears as if Mary is adjusting to the program and the group. Mary really likes getting her rewards and I noticed by her body language that she is much more at ease during group discussions. Please give Mary ten bonus points in the morning for having a good bedtime.

3.   Charting Techniques

Charting systems serve many purposes in programs for troubled youth. Some systems are used as visual reminders to youth that they have received a point or token, completed a task, or advanced to a level of greater independence. Other systems are used by staff to track the frequency of a specific behavior and as reminders to the staff that points were earned, tasks completed and levels acquired. Still other systems are used by staff to keep track of medication dosages, weight and other measurable facts related to a youth's daily care.

The major purposes for the GAP charting system described in this section are to further synthesize observations into useful information and to spot trends in treatment. Child/youth care workers can also use this system to expedite other observing and reporting tasks and as a visual reminder of progress toward treatment goals and objectives. Using the system entails developing criteria for evaluating each youth's daily progress and making evaluations at the end of each shift. For example, the youths in the previous section, John and Mary, may be evaluated as having a below average and an average day respectively. These evaluations can easily be marked on a chart that can be reviewed regularly by all the workers who work with John and Mary.

Following are five techniques for using the GAP charting system:

3.1 **Hold several discussions with fellow team members to determine what constitutes an average day for each youth in relationship to treatment expectations as defined in the treatment plan.** Then determine what constitutes an above average and below average day. Make sure that the criteria are based on consensus and easily observable by all the workers using the charts.

3.2 **Develop a chart with categories for above average, average and below average days.** For example, in the GAP chart depicted in Figure 4, G stands for above average, A for average and P for below average.

3.3 **At the end of each working shift mark the chart according to the evaluation criteria set by the team.** Observational questioning and log notes will help you make an accurate assessment.

3.4 **Review the chart on a regular basis and look for trends or abrupt changes in evaluations.** For example, if a youth has three G days in a row, three P days or a G day followed by a P day and then a G day again, each of these situations may be indicative of a trend or some significant change in the youth's behavior. Once the trend or change is spotted, go back to the log notes and other available information to determine more specifically what might be going on. Then make plans accordingly. For example, if a youth has had two or three bad days, it may be time to plan an activity he/she excels at, have a one to one discussion, or seek new

FIGURE 4 GAP CHART

	1	2	3	4	5	6	7	8	9	10	11	12	13	14	15	16	17	18	19	20	21	22	23	24	25	26	27	28	29	30	31
G	X								X	X								X							X			X			
A		X	X	X		X	X	X			X	X	X	X	X		X		X	X		X	X	X		X	X		X	X	
P					X											X					X										X

support strategies. If a youth is doing well, use more of the same and inform fellow workers about what is working.

3.5 **Prior to major planning meetings summarize findings from the chart in a brief report.** Following are two GAP chart summaries that were substantiated with log notes:

Ex. 1 Jack

G. Only two of 148 days (or 1.3%) were evaluated by the staff as days that exceeded expectations. This was the lowest number of G days for all the six boys studied to date. Correlating information seems to point out that Jack still has a tremendous ability to manipulate his environment so that he does not receive maximum benefit from growth-oriented experiences. Staff members also indicated that they have tremendous difficulty planning activities for Jack.

A. 126 days (or 85%) of the total. There were a large number of average days, but correlated log notes indicated that this was more a matter of going through the motions, of not goofing up, rather than a strong indication of a good investment in treatment. These days almost always occurred during the week when structure was provided.

P. 20 days (or 13.7%) of the total. There were a relatively low number of days in which expectations were not met. The majority of these days (18) occurred on weekends when Jack was more likely to distance himself from adult supervision.

Summary

Although Jack's GAP statistics are not startling, they do seem to disguise a lack of real progress. On the surface Jack has no trouble meeting expectations, yet little change seems to be occurring. Perhaps expectations are too low and motivation lacking. Weekends definitely need more structure for Jack.

Ex. 2 Tim

G. 15 of 127 days (or 11.8%). This seems to be about what was expected for Tim. These days were scattered throughout the week and there did not seem to be a connection with a specific adult or activity. Tim seemed to wake up in a good mood on these days and his attitude seemed to carry throughout the rest of the day.

A. 88 days (or 69.9%). Once again, these days showed no preference for program, adult or day of the week. The correlating log notes indicate a positive attitude for most of the day. One significant factor is that Tim has had only G or A days since being placed in his new school a month ago.

P. 24 (or 18.2%). This is a comparatively high number of days, but 11 of these days were related to illness or a change in staff members. The remaining 13 days were the days in which there were major program changes, such as no school or group outings.

Summary

This evaluation indicates that Tim is responding the way the team expected. He is beginning to adjust to the treatment center, and as long as his day is structured in accordance with his treatment plan, Tim is able to benefit from being here. His extreme dependency seems to show up when the structure breaks down. A future goal might be to help Tim cope better with some of the unpredictables.

3.6 **Use the GAP charting system to provide supportive data for the written reports and recommendations discussed in the next two sections.**

4. Written Report Techniques

In most programs, child/youth care workers are required to prepare written reports of their interactions with a youth over a given period of time, usually a least once every six months. And even in programs where child/youth care workers are not required to submit written reports some form of verbal report is required in order to assess the significance of their involvement with youths. The techniques in this section can help in each of these processes.

Following are four techniques for writing reports:

4.1 **Use major observational questioning categories, technique 1.1, to develop an outline for the report.** For example, you may plan to have at least one paragraph or more for each category in your observational questioning list which is particularily relevant to your interactions with the youth.

4.2 **Review log notes, treatment plans, charts and any additional information that is available.** Take notes while reviewing these materials and code your notes according to the outline. In other words, if notes belong under the heading of Supportive Techniques or Daily Living Routines, code the note according to the number given these categories in the outline.

After all the materials have been reviewed and notes written, go through one last observation questioning process and write down any additional significant thoughts that come to mind. This will serve as the final review before beginning to write the report.

4.3 **Use the outline and the notes to write a draft of the report or to organize a verbal report.** The following report was written by a child/youth care worker who had learned to use thechniques 4.1 and 4.2. Please note that only information which is relevant to this specific youth's treatment plan is reported. The worker did not attempt to put down everything he knew about the youth. He was able to assess which observations and interactions were important and to offer relevant interpretations. These are keys to good written reports.

Jon

Over the past six months, I have noticed several significant changes in Jon. These changes have not been big changes, but a series of smaller changes, which together appear to indicate that Jon is getting ready to become more independent. For example, since our last review I feel Jon has taken more interest and shows greater skill in combing his hair, washing his face, taking a shower and putting away his toys. This growth can mainly be attributed to the one-to-one attention he receives for performing these tasks and the incentive built into the group grooming program. Hopefully in the next six months we will be able to make Jon more aware of the intrinsic value of performing grooming tasks. A more noticeable area of change is Jon's eating habits. His appetite is much more hearty and his table manners have improved significantly. Once again, growth can be attributed to adult support and encouragement, but in this area Jon also seems to be personally enjoying food much more.

Retention continues to be a problem for Jon. He still will hold back despite the obvious discomfort that goes along with not using the toilet. I feel the problem is emotionally and not physically based. Retention usually occurs when Jon is depressed about home or on a home visit. Jon usually retains for his entire home visit, because he is afraid his parents will punish him severely for soiling his shorts. He usually returns on Sunday night in quite a bit of discomfort.

Jon's physical health is generally very good, but he does at times psych himself into being sick and this is also a convenient way to avoid stressful days in school. A review of the group chart and school logs indicates a strong correlation between illness and the introduction of new learning materials.

If Jon is not motivated to participate he will go to extremes to avoid group activities. He will intimidate weakers boys, sluggishly go through the motions or passively resist by hiding in his room. Jon also regresses to thumb sucking in these situations. I feel these behaviors are primarily defenses against trying something new or interacting with others in unfamiliar situations. Much of the anxiety Jon experiences is associated with his feeling of inadequacy in these situations. Thus, he still feels it is more rewarding to get negative attention from adults and peers for resisting, than it is to risk trying to get positive feedback for making an effort to participate. Yet if the adult is very encouraging and expectations are realistic Jon will respond. I find that if I plan in advance and am aware of the activities that create the most stress, particularly team sports and bike riding, I can concentrate on preparing Jon in advance. Once involved, he usually is able to enjoy himself.

Positive changes in social behavior have been made in several areas. Jon is making better eye contact and showing more facial expression. Participation in group activities, especially arts and crafts, music and table games has increased and he is able to accomplish routines as long as he has adult encouragement. I view him as a child with a huge void waiting to be filled with developmentally appropriate activities. It is best to keep these activities reality oriented, because Jon slips into fantasy quite easily. Jon is also developing a close relationship with his roommate. There appears to be a real sense of caring and sharing developing.

Jon's perceptual and gross motor abilities have definitely improved. He can catch and throw a ball much better than last year. His skills on the balance beam have also improved. This improvement has increased his willingness to participate in athletic activities. He is less afraid that he will fail and more aware that this type of involvement can be enjoyable.

I find working with Jon both frustrating and rewarding. The key in our relationship seems to be advanced planning and extra encouragement. If I keep expectations within his capabilities and offer support before, during and after we interact or participate in group activities, Jon responds quite positively. If I become insensitive or frustrated with his lack of progress, Jon can very easily slip into a state of passive resistance. Change is often minimal, but each step is significant for Jon.

4.4 **Put your original draft away for a few days and then go back and write the final report.** Objectivity and accuracy can often be increased by stepping back for a few days.

5. Recommending Techniques

The course of treatment is often shaped by the recommendations that team members make at planning and problem solving meetings. For example, the worker who recommended that Jack (Ex. 1, technique 3.5) needed more structure on weekends may have presented this recommendation to his fellow team members at a planning meeting and they may have decided to adopt, adapt or reject the worker's recommendation. If the recommendation were accepted, it would become part of the treatment plan and change the direction of treatment. Thus, child/youth care workers who make recommendations can be instrumental in determining the nature of future interactions with youths. Recommendations are not always accepted, but the worker who initiates change is more likely to influence final decisions than the worker who constantly reacts to fellow team members' recommendations.

Following are three recommending techniques:

5.1 **While writing logs, written reports or going through the observational questioning process, try to formulate recommendations which will create positive change for a given youth.** Use the data collected while using the previous techniques as support for recommendations. For example, the following recommendations were attached to the written report presented in the previous section.

Recommendations

1. A special program should be designed to reinforce Jon for appropriately using the toilet and for not retaining. The best reinforcers would be a chart with stars and special one-to-one attention with significant male workers.

2. We should all encourage a more consistent performance on the group's grooming program.

3. Jon should also be encouraged to be more direct in his expression of feelings.

4. Whenever Jon sucks his thumb the adults should quietly bring this to his attention. This should be done away from the group. Thumb sucking will probably decrease as his self-concept increases, but in the meantime it won't hurt to make him aware of when he's doing it.

5. More high interest activities should be planned (i.e., arts and crafts, music, and table games) and Jon should be enrolled in our school's special physical education class.

6. Power struggles should be avoided, but pressure can be increased for Jon to take more responsibility for his own routine care. Perhaps a program can be designed to relate his ability to take more responsibility in this area with greater independence during free time.

5.2 **Whenever the team gets together to discuss problems or design treatment plans, come prepared with at least a couple of recommendations for change.** Additional recommendations may come to mind during the meeting, but it is best to have several in mind before the meeting starts.

5.3 **Be prepared to compromise.** It is always helpful to have an alternative recommendation to replace the original recommendation. Teams of workers seldom accept a recommendation without modifications. This is a natural part of the consensus decision-making process.

6. Summarizing Techniques

Most programs for troubled youth have treatment plan summaries which are attached to youths' records and handed out to team members for constant reference. Summaries usually highlight the essential components of the treatment plan to be carried out over a given period of time. The summary can be altered during this time period, but major changes usually are not made until the next formal planning meeting.

Summaries vary from program to program, but most summaries include at least three general sections or parts: target behaviors, reasons or purposes for behavior, and behavior change or intervention strategies. The **target behavior section** identifies the inappropriate and appropriate behaviors the team wants to prevent, support or correct. The **reason or purpose section** briefly identifies or describes the underlying reasons and purposes for the behaviors, and the **strategies section** describes the type of action the team will take to reach the desired results.

All summaries are references to guide child/youth care workers' daily interactions. Thus, no worker should be without some type of treatment plan summary for each youth in his/her group, even workers who work with youth for only a short period of time.

Following are two summarizing techniques:

6.1   **If the agency does not have a summary format, develop a simple summary to review daily.** The following summary is a simplified example of a basic summary.

Sam
TARGET BEHAVIORS
Negative Behaviors
1. Manipulation of peers and adults bribes and threats.
2. Unrealistic verbal exaggerations of accomplishments.
3. Temper tantrums.
4. Poor grooming habits.
5. Poor male identification.
6. Poor learning skills.
7. Doesn't pay attention in school distracts others.
8. Avoids physically active group activities.

Positive Behaviors
1. Has leadership capabilities.
2. Verbally sophisticated.
3. Good coordination.
4. Knows how to act age appropriately if he wants to.
5. Has good retention skills in the classroom.

PURPOSE OR REASON FOR BEHAVIOR

To hide his own insecurities about unfamiliar adults in a leadership position. To maintain fantasy image he has of his father.

To avoid experiences in which his capabilities can't meet his unrealisitc self-expectations.

BEHAVIOR CHANGE PROGRAMS

1. Channel strengths into a positive leadership role.
   Example: group discusssions.
2. Involve Sam in age-appropriate activities de-emphasizing competitive and comparative situations.
3. Use appropriate logical consequences and avoid verbal power struggles.
4. Don't play down fantasies or exaggerations in front of group.
5. Lead by example rather than by criticism.
6. Place him on group grooming program.
7. Begin charting activity involvement. Head toward goal of greater independence; until then provide normal supervision.
8. Casework will provide one-to-one to strengthen male indentity.
9. Family sessions will concentrate on family system — all membes will participate.

10. Father can be invited to participate with Sam in weekend group activity.
11. Sam will be placed on individual reading program in school.
12. Attempts to distract others in school will be dealt with verbally and with short time outs in school setting (made up after school).
13. Praise Sam on the living unit for good days in school.

6.2 **End each day or shift with a review of the summary for each youth and make notations or recommendations for improving or changing the summary on an attached sheet of paper.** Then present the recommendations and suggestions at the next planning meeting. This is the best way to keep the summary updated and to assure that it is prescribing a direction which will meet the youths' ever changing treatment needs.

Summary

Observing and reporting are vital aspects of the child/youth care worker's role. When workers can articulate their observations and make recommendations based on these observations, they are one step ahead in the intervention process, because future direct interventions will be based on a firsthand awareness and understanding of the problems. The techniques presented in this chapter and similar techniques can aid child/youth care workers with their observing and reporting tasks. These tasks are never easy, but over the long run time spent on becoming an objective observer and reporter can pay off in increased confidence, competence, and effective treatment plans.

CHAPTER THREE

GROUP ACTIVITY TECHNIQUES

Group activity techniques are the organizational procedures child/youth care workers use to increase the potential for successful group activities. Child/youth care workers usually spend most of their time involved in some form of group activity such as daily living routines, recreational and vocational activities, group meetings or discussions and community outings. When group activitiy techniques are used to select, prepare and conduct activities which meet individual and group treatment, there are few alternatives which play a more significant role in treating troubled youths.

The focus in this chapter is on organizational as opposed to interactive aspects of group activites, not because the interactive aspect is less important, but because positive group interaction usually ensues from good organization. The interactive aspects of group activities will be discussed in the following chapters. All of the techniques in this chapter are preventive or supportive techniques designed to promote positive group activities. The techniques include:

1. Coordinating
2. Transitioning
3. Selecting
4. Group Discussions
5. Planning
6. Organizing

7. Activity Guidelines

7. Coordinating Techniques

When several groups live in the same environments or interact on a regular basis, child/youth care workers must coordinate their efforts to avoid daily chaos. Groups of troubled youth do not automatically get along together or blend together in cohesive movement through the treatment environment. Intra group interactions as well as group independence are contingent upon the ability of workers to recognize the factors that will enhance or deter productive group coexistence.

The following coordination techniques will be helpful in programs where there are two or more groups.

7.1 **Hold planning meetings for workers who work the same shift or who are in charge of groups during the same time of the day.** The focus of these meetings should be on discussing factors which will enhance group coexistence. These factors, as shall be seen in the following example, can then be outlined for easy daily reference.

7.2 **Break the day or shift into specific time periods and list behaviors or guidelines which each worker can follow in order to promote positive group involvement.** For example, the following schedule was developed by a group of child/youth care workers who worked the same shift. This schedule may not necessarily be appropriate for your setting, but it is indicative of the type of specificity which is needed.

2:55 — End of School Day

1. Be available to pick up your group as they are excused from school.
2. Keep doors unlocked.
3. Have an afternoon treat in the TV room.
4. Have supplies or equipment for the group ready.

3:00-4:45 — Mid-Afternoon Activity

1. Keep boys out of hall.
2. Use your TV room as a gathering area for those who have changed their school clothes.
3. Establish cohesion in the group before leaving the TV room.
4. Do not leave unattended boys behind. It is preferred that you wait until the whole group has arrived from school before leaving the unit. If it is impossible to do this, then be sure that another group worker has accepted responsibility for the boys left behind.
5. The afternoon treat should be available at three o'clock.
6. Don't monopolize an activity area with one boy. This is a time when activity areas should be available for groups.
7. This is activity time. The time can be spent in groups or as a free period depending on the decision of the

working team. Some supervision of all boys is necessary. Each group leader should know where his boys are and what they are doing. Coverage of activity areas during free period should be coordinated through the person in charge.

4:45 p.m. — Wash and Quiet

1. Have your group wash hands, and quiet down in the TV room for the transition to a quiet meal.
2. Groups who eat later should be out of the hall and starting their rest period after the other groups go down to supper.

5:00-5:30 — Supper

5:30-6:30 Rest Period

1. Boys should spend the rest period in their rooms or in the TV room.
2. Boys should not be in the hall.
3. Determine the need for supplies, help with homework, etc., with your group members at the beginning of the rest period, and provide them as you deem appropriate.
4. Group workers should check on the individuals in their group about every fifteen minutes, or as often as necessary.
5. Boys should not be allowed to call their group worker or come to the office to ask questions. Questions may be asked when the group worker checks on his or her boys in their rooms.

6. Activity and noise level should be kept low.
7. Take a break, coordinate use of equipment and activity areas and prepare for the evening activity. This is probably the best opportunity for the working team to communicate during the evening shift.

6:30 — End of Rest Period: Gathering for Group

1. Use your TV room or one of the boys' rooms to gather before starting your evening group activity. Do not congregate in the hall!
2. For the boys, the rest period ends when they are excused by their group leader.
3. For the staff, rest period ends at 6:30, and they should be prompt in picking up their groups.

6:30-8:30 — Evening Activity and Showers: See Activity Standards

1. Keep groups separate unless they are together by plan.
2. In bringing groups up for activity, avoid walking through areas where other groups are, especially on the living unit.
3. Working teams should arrange showering schedules.

8:00-8:30 — Wind Down Time

1. 8:00 — Hall and sink area lights should be out. TV room doors should be kept closed.
2. 8:30 — Showers should be completed

unless the boys who have yet to shower can do so quietly. Some boys may be in bed. Unnecessary traffic and noise in the hall should cease.

8:30-10:30 —
Quiet Time: Transition to Bedtime

1. Prepare for the transisition to bedtime before entering the hall. Establish quiet, calm order.
2. Have individuals use the toilet and get a drink, one or two at a time, before they go to bed. Dispense medication and get extra blankets immediately, not after bedtime.
3. Boys should be taught to wait in their rooms for you to come by, rather than seek you in hall or elsewhere.
4. Stay near your group's rooms at least until all members of the group are settled. At this time, control and quiet are a first priority. Log writing and personal attention to group members should be attempted only after control and quiet are established.
5. Radios should be kept low.
6. Remain on duty until your group is settled and until your assigned tasks are completed. Each working team will divide areas of daily responsibility among its members. It is the responsibility of each worker to see his assumed area is kept clean and in order. Examples are: the unit kitchen, the child care workers' office, the recreation room, the

art room, etc.

10:30 p.m.

Inform the night watchmen of anything they should be aware of regarding a particular boy, or anything significant which may have a bearing on the evening. Examples:

1. Behavior or anxiety problems.
2. Illness or other health concerns.
3. The number of boys present.

7.3 **Have copies of the daily schedule made and circulate copies to all the workers.** This schedule will serve as the daily guide to group interaction. It can and should be modified on a regular basis to meet the current needs of groups.

8. Transitioning Techniques

Movement to and from group activities can be as important as the actual activity. If group members arrive at an activity in lousy shape or leave an activity without a proper sense of closure, the value of the activity can be drastically reduced. If group members start out on a positive note and feel good about how the activity ends, then the probability that the activity will succeed is vastly increased.

Following are four transitioning techniques:

8.1 **When planning group activities, include enough time to begin and end the activity.** The time will vary according to the activity. For example, ten minutes for a one-hour art and crafts activity may be needed to clean-up and get ready to leave the room. A game of basketball may require only five minutes to settle the group down at the end, but perhaps ten minutes to get everyone to change their shoes in the beginning. There are any number of additional factors to consider with each activity. The point is to remember that part of every activity period must be set aside to begin and end the activity.

8.2 **Look carefully at how one activity affects another activity.** For example, if the activity preceding bedtime involves physical activity, don't expect to rush right into bedtime. Leave plenty of time for the group to settle down. If the group has been cooped up for a period of time, an outdoor activity may be appropriate, but don't expect everyone to suddenly be ready to move from a closed to open environment. Bring the group together and get a feel for the group's readiness to change environments, then move ahead at the proper pace. Once again there are any number of possible considerations to explore. The objectives, therefore, are to realize that the activity level of one activity influences another and to plan accordingly.

8.3 **Bring the group together as a unit before moving from one activity to another.** This can be a difficult task, but it is important for the group to get used to moving together. There are too many possibiliites for negative interactions when groups move about in a fragmented fashion. When the group is being brought together, do not line the youths up single file. The purpose for coming together is to have everyone who will be involved in the upcoming activity standing or sitting in a space in which you can easily observe everyone, not to creat a military atmosphere. If the group members are in good shape then move on to the next activity. If they are not, settle things down before moving on.

8.4 **With some youths, it may be helpful to describe the next activity before moving on.** This may reduce some of their anxiety about what is going to happen to them next.

9. Selecting Techniques

Selecting the right types of activities for individual members of the group and the group as a whole is the most important activity technique. Productive activities don't "just happen." Each activity requires forethought and planning. One of the major problems with programs for youths is that not enough energy is put into selecting appropriate activities for a specific population of youths. For example, troubled youths are often forced to play team sports such as basketball and baseball day after day, even though the group has trouble playing these games together. The assumption is that things will get better with more practice. However, when one examines the group members' individual strengths and weaknesses, it may become apparent that a team sport is the last thing the group should be playing. Several of the youths may lack the sophisticated skills which are required to hit and catch a baseball, or bounce and shoot a basketball. Others may not have the emotional and social strengths which are required to cooperate as team members. Consequently, the group continues to fail time after time. This situation calls for a better selection of activities, not more practice. The group could be playing less sophisticated games which teach group members how to develop the skills required to play team sports in the future.

The activity selecting techniques in this section can be used to select activities which are not a set part of the program. Set activities include group grooming programs, mealtimes, regularly scheduled recreation periods and vocational classes which the team has determined are essential for the group to participate in on a regular basis. These activities will be discussed in later chapters. The techniques in this section will help workers select activities for the many time periods in which they must use their own ingenuity and creativity to keep the group productively involved together.

Following are five activity selecting techniques:

9.1 **Develop a list of activities for each youth in the group.** The list should include several activities which are appropriate for a youth's various levels of development. For example, a music activity for a youth with musical talents or youths who need an alternative form of expression, a balance activity for youths with perceptual motor and coordination difficulties, and community outings for youths who need to develop appropriate social skills. Suggestions for appropriate activities can be obtained from the treatment plan, fellow team members and hundreds of references at the library (see the bibliography for some suggested activity readings).

9.2 **Develop a group activity list by identifying activities which appear on each of the individual activity lists.** This approach will help assure that group activities meet the needs of all group members. For example, the group activity list in Figure 5 is based on common activities identified in the lists for Jerry and Pete.

9.3 **Develop lists for subgroupings.** There will be several activities which meet the needs of only a few group members, but these activities should not be overlooked. By listing these activities you can create a ready reference for those times when you are involved with only a few group members and looking for an appropriate activity.

9.4 **Use these lists to prepare an activity planner (see 11 Activity Planning Techniques).**

9.5 **In short term programs, develop lists which include the general types of**

Figure 5 Activity Lists*

Jerry:

- Four Square
- Pottery
- Simple Woodworking
- Raking Leaves
- Shoveling Snow
- Track and Field — running and high jump
- Grocery Shopping
- Trips to Fire Station, Police, etc.
- Singing
- Kickball
- Hiking
- Cross Country Skiing
- Cooking — simple items, i.e., popcorn
- Table Games and cards and checkers
- Balance Beam Exercises

Pete:

- Advanced Woodworking
- Four Square
- Basketball
- Auto Mechanics
- Raking Leaves
- Shoveling Snow
- Track and Field — all events
- Trips to Record Store, Social Center, etc.
- Cooking — popcorn
- Hiking
- Cross Country Skiing
- Swimming
- Gymnastics
- Table Games — all types
- Track and Field — all events

Group Activities:

Four Square
Woodworking
Raking Leaves
Shoveling Snow
Track and Field
Hiking
Cross Country Skiing
Table Games
Cooking — Popcorn

Leisure Time

Bob — Table Games
Jake — Sand Box Puzzles
John — Bike Riding, Volleyball, Reading
Tim — Model Building, Practice Piano, Horse Shoes
Jerry — Jogging, Work in Garden

*These are sample lists. Most groups will have six to eight youths and consequently the group list will be longer. Individual lists may also be consider-

65

activities that will benefit the youth in the program. It may not be possible to develop comprehensive lists such as the ones suggested above, but some form of list should be created for regular references.

10. Group Discussion Techniques

Group discussion techniques are presented in several parts of the book. In each instance, group discussions are characterized as catalysts or excellent sources of information for selecting intervention techniques. The group discussion techniques presented here can be used as catalysts for successful activity periods.

Following are three group discussion techniques.

10.1 **Provide plenty of opportunity for troubled youth to discuss activities as a group.** They can evaluate current activities and make suggestions for future activities. The adult usually makes the final decision about which activities are added or subtracted from the activity list, but the youths' impressions about activities will assist the adults in making effective decisions.

10.2 **Allow the group ample opportunity to choose its own activities from the activity list** (emphasis is placed on the activity list, because the assumption is that if an activity meets the youths' treatment needs it should be on the list). The decision-making process will have to be guided by the adult, but group member involvement in making activity decisions increases probabilities for activity success and group cohesion.

10.3 **Try to hold group decision-making sessions far in advance of an activity and to make involvement in the activity contingent upon successful completion of preceding activities.** Last minute decision-making can lead to poor selections and groups which are not cooperating in required or preceding activities are less likely to do very well in activities of their own choosing.

11. Activity Planning Techniques

Child/youth care workers usually have a considerable amount of freedom and independence in selecting when and how activities are conducted, because they work in a somewhat open ended environment. They are not confined to classrooms or offices, nor are they totally bound by clocks or specific daily schedules. These can be tremendous advantages if workers are astute in matching group activites to group motivation. In other words, they can often conduct an activity when the group is ready and not necessarily when their schedules dictate they must have an activity. Of course, some activities are scheduled for a specific time and place, but in general child/youth care workers do have the luxury of having more flexibility than most other youth care professionals.

Flexible conditions, however, require perhaps even more preplanning than less flexible conditions. In order to utilize flexibility, one must always have a variety of alternatives available. Without alternatives chaos or unproductive activity will usually ensue. For example, workers who allow their groups to "do their own thing" most of the time will either spend a great deal of time involved in crisis intervention or in extremely passive activities such as watching TV. On the other hand, workers with activity alternatives for a variety of occasions will usually have very positive group experiences. Hence, activity planning is equally important to child/youth care workers as it is to all other youth care professionals.

Following are nine activity planning techniques:

11.1 **Prepare an activitiy planner with three sections; a section for listing several potential activities and scheduled activities for a given period of time; a section for activity goals; and a section for a critical analysis or evaluation of each activity.** (see Figure 6)

11.2 **List enough activities to cover a reasonable period of time, perhaps one week.** Use activity lists, techniques 9.1 and 9.2 for suggestions.

11.3 **List the goals for each activity.** Goals may include both individual and group goals. Individual goals are based on treatment plans and articulated or further identified during the activity selecting process. Group goals can be determined through discussions with fellow team members. For example, one group may want to stress group unity, another prepare for an upcoming event such as a camping trip and still another may be working on subgroup activities.

11.4 **Always include time for leisure activities and planned group discussions about activities.** Several suggestions for leisure time activities for each youth can be taken from the activity lists and attached to the planner. Advance group discussions will give the youths an opportunity to make their own activity decisions in a productive organized fashion, rather than at the last minute.

11.5 **Include a few subgroup activities which can be employed when an opportunity is presented.** Subgroup activities can be taken from activity lists 9.3.

11.6 **Review the activity planner at the beginning of each working shift.** Then jot down on a small note card the time and names of scheduled activities and list three or four alternative activities which match the individual and group needs for that day or shift. Needs can be determined by reviewing logs and charts, techniques 2 and 3.

11.7 **At a convenient time, analyze completed activities.** It is usually best to do this as soon after the activity as possible, but it may be more convenient to wait till the end of the shift when you may have time to sit down and think.

Figure 6

Activity	Goals	Analysis
Four Square	To give each child a chance to participate in a group game emphasizing individual skills. This is an especially good game for Bob and Jake who need to work on hand/eye coordination.	Everyone enjoyed the game. The pace was just right. 45 minutes seems to be the best length of time. Interest is still high, but energy levels are low. It is good to have a quiet game to follow. Bob and Jake each seem to be hitting the ball better.
Ceramics	The group has not used clay lately. John has special talent in this area and he needs an opportunity to express it. The rest of the group should be able to handle this media. Hopefully, everyone can make something worthwhile for their rooms.	John as usual did very well. He made a paper weight for his desk. The rest of the group could not handle the stimulus. They began throwing the clay. In the future, projects should be spelled out and firmer rules established before the groups enter the arts and crafts rooms.

Three hours of group choice	To pursue the group decision making process. Emphasis will be placed on encouraging all the boys to actively participate.	Although the activities chosen (bike riding, hiking and fishing) were appropriate, they were too much to accomplish in one week. The group will have to be steered towards more realistic goals in future or the choices should be limited by the types of activities chosen. Everyone except Tim participated.
Perceptual Motor Special Group Thurs. 4:00-5:00 Balance Beam	Concentration will be on forward and backward walking. The four inch balance beam will be used.	Harry is still frightened going backwards. The rest of the group is o.k. We will have to move on. Perhaps Harry's child care workers can give him individual help so he doesn't fall too far behind.

11.8 **Use the critical analysis section to update activity lists.** You may want to eliminate activities which are not working well, accentuate successful activities, or search for new activities.

11.9 **If you have the time and energy, it is beneficial to develop an activity booklet which includes descriptions and analyses of the many activities you have used.** This booklet can be a very helpful part of your own professional growth and an invaluable aid to fellow workers.

12. Organizing Techniques

Each activity requires a certain amount of organization. Materials might have to be prepared, time allotted, space reserved and cleaning articles acquired. Some activities such as kickball require only minimal organization — getting the ball and reserving the space in the gym or outside. Others such as making papier maché require considerable more organization — ordering supplies, reserving space, setting up and clean up. Regardless of how much organization is required, it is equally as important as the other organizational factors. Poorly organized activities can be expected to fail the same as poorly selected or planned activities.

Following are five organizing techniques:

12.1 **At some point in advance of the activity, usually the beginning of a shift, make sure that the materials** needed to conduct the activity are laid aside in a convenient location. There is nothing more frustrating and/or upsetting than to find out at the start of an activity that materials are not available. For example, if the balls are all being used or there is a shortage of arts and crafts materials, group cohesion will quickly deteriorate.

12.2 **Reserve the space you will need to conduct the activity far in advance.** The same problems can arise when adequate space is not available as when materials are not available.

12.3 **Select a proper space to accommodate the activity.** The space in which an activity is conducted is extremely important to activity success. For example, messy arts and craft projects or auto mechanics are not usually conducted in the group's TV room.

12.4 **Prepare the space to accommodate the activity.** Even when the proper space is selected, further organization may be required to assure activity success. For example, for some groups it may be best to reduce the stimuli such as having only one ball for the kickball game or having only papier maché supplies out in the arts and crafts room in order to facilitate concentration on the tasks at hand. Other activities such as leisure time activities and creative expressive activities may rely upon having extra stimuli in order to encourage participation.

12.5 **Take the necessary steps to have whatever is needed to clean up available when the activity is completed.** Clean up is as much a part of a successful activity period as is the actual activity.

13. Activity Guideline Techniques

It is often very beneficial for a team of workers to agree upon some basic guidelines which can be applied to selective activity areas such as physical education and creative expressive activities. These guidelines like other guidelines can provide a foundation for selecting and planning activities. Activity guidelines should not, however, stifle individual youths' rights to meaningful activities or discourage worker creativity and innovation. The task is to be as general as possible, highlighting only those activity characteristics which the team feels will enhance activity success.

Following are two activity guideline techniques:

13.1 **Conduct a series of team meetings for the purpose of identifying activity guidelines.** The guideline process can be improved significantly by including youths in various aspects of the discussion.

13.2 **List the guidelines which are established by the team.** Following is one set of guidelines: Once again, these guidelines may not be appropriate for your setting, but the contents are indicative of the kind of effort which is required.

Team Game Guidelines

1. De-emphasize winning, losing and team or individual competition. Emphasize the individual as a part of a team effort and encourage or praise self improvement and cooperative efforts which are compatible with individual strengths and weaknesses.

2. Work up to more sophisticated team sports such as basketball, baseball, football, soccer and ice hockey by first exposing the group to a series of lead-up activities such as kickball, bounce and run, huddle run and basic ice skating.

3. Alternate team games with games or activities which accentuate individual achievements such as track and field events. Once again encourage and reward group members for individual efforts, not comparative achievements.

4. Use subgroups for youths who have specific strengths or weaknesses with team games.

Summary

Successful group activities are usually the results of considerable pre-thought and planning. The planning, selecting and preparing techniques presented in this chapter can help expedite the organizational process. However, these techniques, like observing and reporting techniques, require time and practice to master, time which must often come at the workers' own expense. But over the long run, most child/youth workers' are more self satisfied and effective in their jobs if they have developed effective organizational activity skills. Workers who rely totally on instinct or spontaneous group interventions are usually frustrated and ineffective.

CHAPTER FOUR

REINFORCEMENT TECHNIQUES

Reinforcement is the additional support or assistance child/youth workers provide for troubled youths to get involved in growing experiences. Troubled youths require extra reinforcement such as praise, encouragement, positive peer reinforcement, rewards and privileges, because they lack sufficient internal reinforcement or self motivation to grow. For example, troubled youths often need constant praise and encouragement to complete routine daily tasks such as combing their hair or playing a game with peers, because they do not receive sufficient self satisfaction from completing these tasks for themselves. As they progress in the program many of these tasks may become more self satisfying, but until they reach that point they need all the outside help they can get.

The immediate purpose for each of the techniques presented in this chapter is to provide additional support and assistance for troubled youths to get involved in the ongoing activity. The ultimate purpose, however, is to increase their intrinsic or internal motivation to grow by reinforcing them to get involved in situations which can help improve their feelings and perceptions about themselves.

The reinforcement techniques in this chapter are titled:

1. Praise
2. Encouragement

3. Positive Peer Reinforcement
4. Reward Systems
5. Privilege Systems

Reinforcement Guidlines

In this chapter and the next, guidelines which are based on the assessment areas outlined in Chapter One will be presented prior to specific techniques. The guidelines will serve to remind the reader that there are basic criteria which must be considered before using the direct intervention techniques described in each chapter. The following guidelines can be applied to using reinforcement techniques:

1. **The diagnostic section of the treatment plan should be used to set realistic expectations.** Reinforcement techniques are effective when expectations are realistic. Expectations are usually based on the youth's current stages of emotional, cognitive and physical development as defined in the treatment plan by the workers and their fellow team members. The objectives are to determine expectations which are not too high or too low for these stages. For example, workers who want to reward a youth for verbal expression of feelings when nonverbal expression is all the youth is currently capable of, or workers who are praising a youth every time the hammer hits the head of the nail when the youth already knows how to drive a nail, are going to be reinforcing the wrong behaviors. On the other hand, workers who are encouraging youth with budding

artistic talents to draw a mural for the group Thanksgiving party will have greater success.

2. **The target behavior section of the treatment plan, technique 6, should be used to identify specific behaviors to support or reinforce.** The target behavior section or a similar part of the treatment can provide helpful answers to the following questions: What is it that you are trying to reinforce the youth for doing? or What specific behaviors are you trying to support or reinforce? If the answers to these questions are "be a nice guy," or "appropriate social behaviors," workers will not have much success. These answers are to diffuse and unclear. On the other hand, if the answers are reward him/her for saying, "hi, how are you," or "praise him/her for combing his/her hair in the morning before breakfast," workers are more likely to succeed.

3. **Relationships should be assessed before using relevant techniques.** Relationships play a key role in determining which reinforcement technique to use. For example, praise, encouragement and positive peer reinforcement are contingent upon the youth's desire to please adults and/or peers. If youths do not want to or are not ready to please others, the potential for these techniques is minimized. Privileges, on the other hand, require trusting relationships. Without trusting relationships it is almost

impossible to make appropriate assessments for advancement within a privilege system. Rewards, however do not necessarily require trusting or pleasing relationships. Consequently, workers often use rewards before using other techniques.

4. **Every technique should be evaluated in relationship to the environmental factors which will enhance or deter implementation.** Workers need to know whether a technique can be effectively implemented before trying to use it to reinforce behavior. At least three major factors should be considered. First, the behavior must be observable. All the workers who are going to use the technique must be able to observe the desired behavior on a regular basis. Second, the system must be manageable. If rewards are to be handed out, charts marked, or privileges monitored, each worker must be able to effectively integrate these tasks into his/her daily workload. Finally, workers must be able to employ the technique during or as soon after a desired behavior as possible. Reinforcement techniques lose effectiveness when implementation is delayed, missed or forgotten. The sooner the technique is implemented the better it will work.

14. Praise

Praise is social reinforcement which is

motivating to youth who want to please adults and peers. It is one of the most common reinforcement techniques, because it is based on positive statements about behavior. Praise is also very easy to use. All it requires are a few positive comments from the adult at the right time. Hence, most child/youth workers use praise several times each day.

While praise is an extremely important and effective technique, there are three precautions that have been raised in the past few years which are worth mentioning. First, praise is used with the completion of tasks and troubled youth are not very good at completing of tasks. If it is used alone, or it is the only technique, youths can get the message that they are only good when they complete tasks and this probably will not happen often enough to be productive. Therefore, praise frequently needs to be combined with encouragement in order to be effective.[1]

Second, praise can be detrimental if it is used as a value judgment or an attempt to set up the youth for some ulterior motive.[2] For example, the worker who heaps on the praise and then asks a youth to double his workload the next day is abusing praise. Finally, praise often creates a "Madison Avenue" or unrealistic image of a youth, which can be destructive if the youth is not prepared.[3] Troubled youths generally have very poor self images and if praise conveys an image which is too positive or extreme, the youths may act out to show their true selves.

Following are five praise techniques:

14.1 **Checkout relationship with team-mates.** Praise requires a desire to please adults or earn their praise. It is important, therefore, that you are fairly certain that this type of relationship exists between you and the youth before relying upon praise to do the job. This doesn't mean that you can't praise most of the youths, but praise should not be relied upon as a primary technique if your relationship has not reached the point where the youth wants to please you.

14.2 **Make sure praise is appropriate for the current situation.** The following example describes how a worker can be set up to use praise inappropriately:

Bill and Jim were supposed to be doing their homework, but instead were building a model together in Bill's room. Actually, Jim was doing most of the work, because he was the better model builder. Along came a worker from another unit. Bill quickly grabbed the model from Jim and ran up to the worker saying, "Look at the new model I just built. Isn't it nice?" The worker replied, "Boy, that's nice, I really like that." Then the original worker returned to see how the homework was coming.

These situations can be avoided by taking the time to ask questions and by checking things out with fellow workers. This may require making statements such as, "I'd like to look at it a little later," or "I'm not sure that I should be talking with you now; let me check and then come back."

14.3 **Avoid statements which exaggerate or embellish accomplishments.** For example, try to avoid the following statements: "You're such a great guy, that's the best I've ever seen,"; "I'm so happy you did that. You're really wonderful."; "You're so sharp, you did exactly what I asked."; "I'm so pleased that you did that just for me."; "You always do the best job."; "That's so good, I can't see why you can't do that every time."; "You're my best helper."; "Every time you try that project, you always do so much better than I expected." These comments create unrealistic images of the youth and can convey the message that your expectations are much higher than the youth's expectations of himself/herself.

14.4 **Praise a situation as it stands and check to see if the youth's perceptions and feelings are the same as yours.** The following statements and comments may be appropriate: "That appears to be a difficult accomplishment. How did you achieve it?"; "I like your hair that way. How do you feel about keeping it combed?"; "I feel good about our effort on this project. How do you feel?"; "I enjoyed building this windmill with you. Let me know when you are ready to try again."; "Your room was dirty. I think it is a lot better now. What do you think?";

"You don't look happy about your drawing. I think it'sbetter than your last one, but I guess you don't?"; "I am glad you could say that. Do you feel better about it now?" These statements are directed at specific situations and give the youth the impression that it is O.K. to feel differently.

14.5 **Use praise spontaneously whenever it is obvious that you feel good about the accomplishments.** The above techniques suggest that praise usually needs some forethought and knowledge of the youth and what's going on. There will, however, be many situations where personal instincts will indicate that it's perfectly reasonable to go ahead and praise a youth.

15. Encouragement

Encouragement is also social reinforcement that is effective with youths who want to please. However, encouragement is used while youths are trying, even when they try and fail. The essence of encouragement is to increase youths' confidence in themselves and to convey a message that they are good as they are and not just as they might be.[4]

Following are three encouragement techniques:

15. **Offer reassurance, but recognize that a youth may not be ready to try at that point.** The objective is to support a pace of growth which is consistent with youths' developmental needs and not your desire to see change occur.

15.2 **Use comments that will reduce rather than increase anxiety about future events.** The following example describes what can happen if precautions are not taken:

John went to his child care worker and said, "I'm nervous about roller skating tonight. There's going to be some girls there; I don't think I want to go." The worker responded, "I'm sure you'll do just fine." John went back to his room and had a temper tantrum. The worker seemed totally surprised. Actually, he shouldn't have been. What he thought was a supportive remark could only add to John's anxiety. John was looking for reassurance that it was okay to be nervous and that someone would be there to lend support if things got out of hand.

The following comments are more appropriate for these situations:

"I can't understand why you feel nervous. This is a new experience for you. I'll tell you what. If you feel uncomfortable at the roller rink I'll be glad to talk with you about it. Just come over to the side and we'll go downstairs together to discuss your feelings." Phrases like "Don't worry about it," or "Everything will be okay" do little to relieve anxiety.

15.3 **If a youth has already failed, try to convey an accepting, calm reassuring attitude.** Your tone of voice and your expression will often determine whether the youth will try again or not. For example, the disgusted-looking adult who shouts, "You goofed again. Won't you ever learn? Let's try again and see if you can't do better," is obviously setting the youth up for continual failure. Instead the adult might very calmly say, "I can see that you feel bad about your mistake, but perhaps something can be learned from this experience. Let's try again together." Other supportive comments are: "I'm willing to give it another try if you are." "Let's try again at a pace you feel comfortable with," and "I know it seems hard, but if we take a closer look it may not be as hard as it seems."

16. Positive Peer Reinforcement

Positive peer reinforcement is additional praise and encouragement coming from one's peers which has an added attraction in that most youths prefer support and recognition from their peers over similar forms of support and recognition from adults. The objective, then, is for the child/youth worker to create an environment in which youths can receive as much positive peer reinforcement as possible. The following example points to the significance of the worker's role in generating positive peer reinforcement:

Phil

Phil was a hyperactive, compulsive child who constantly needed reassurance that the adults would be able to remain in control of his living environment and the group. As an attempt to deal with his feelings of insecurity, Phil continually tried to place himself in an adult role. Phil's peers quickly picked this up and labeled him "office man." It seemed as if nothing the workers did could rid Phil of this image. They often ended up supporting Phil's insecurity, because they became so frustrated with his behavior.

An ingenious child care worker thought he had the answer. Phil obviously had a lot of energy or he wouldn't be able to keep up his constant search for holes in the treatment system. The worker took Phil to the jogging track. He wanted to see if this would help Phil "burn off" some anxiety and he thought perhaps Phil might enjoy distance running. Phil did more than enjoy running; he became the best distance runner in the group. He would get up in the morning and jog around the building to keep in practice. Gradually the group began to see another side of Phil. They stopped looking at him as just an office man and started asking him questions about his running. The experience was maximized at a track meet where Phil had the best individual time in the group.

The significance of this example is not that all of Phil's problems were solved, but that a child care worker was able to involve him in activities where peer interaction could be used to support growth rather than perpetuate a problem. Phil temporarily reached the in-group. This had to be done many more times before he was able to become an accepted group member.

Following are three positive peer reinforcement

techniques.

16.1 **Use activity lists and planners (techniques 9 & 10) to select and plan activities which will provide an opportunity for each youth in your group to succeed at group activities on a regular basis.** In other words, try to create situations where youths can move from their positions as group isolates or followers to the in-group, if for only a short period of time.[5] The in-group is the place within the group where most youths prefer to be. In-group members, are the people who at any given point in time are receiving the most recognition, support and admiration from their peers. A few youths reach this point very naturally, but most will need your help. Selecting and planning the right activity is the best place to start.

16.2 **During an activity, make group members aware of each other's accomplishments.** Youths are sometimes the last ones to recognize that one of their peers has made a significant contribution or achievement. This is not because they are unaware of what's going on, but because in the past they have not received much recognition themselves. Therefore, the adult must often help draw out supportive comments and expressions. This can be rather tricky. You have to be careful not to set the youth up by making it appear as if he/she is receiving special adult attention or preference (this varies with age and developmental levels of the group) and yet, you may need to be fairly obvious or the situation may go unnoticed. Practice is the best solution. However, even practice won't work if an attempt is not being made to try to give each youth an opportunity to reach the in-group at some point or another. It is rather difficult for youths to support their peers if they are not receiving similar support on a regular basis.

16.3 **Hold group discussions with the purpose of pointing out significant accomplishments for each group member over a given period of time, usually every few days.** If every group member is receiving support, then some of the problems presented above can be eliminated. The task here is to be able to identify significant accomplishments for everyone. Once again, the probability of doing this is significantly increased by a good awareness of the treatment plans and effective use of the techniques in the two previous chapters.

17. Reward Systems

Praise, encouragement, and positive peer reinforcement are not always sufficient. Some youths may need more concrete support before these techniques can be effective. In other words, some youths may be motivated by a reward such as a piece of candy or a special activity before they are motivated to please someone. Eventually these youths may want to please others and themselves, but because many troubled youths have not experienced pleasing or self-fulfilling relationships they often need something else in order to get started.

There are two general types of rewards, primary rewards and secondary rewards. Primary rewards are defined here as rewards that satisfy basic biological needs such as food, water, clothing, shelter and sleep. These rewards are a natural part of a treatment program and, therefore, youths should not have to earn or be deprived of these rewards under any circumstances. Secondary rewards can be a material item such as a piece of fruit, money or a token earned toward a special item such as a model car kit, or social activities such as going to the store or spending one to one time with an adult playing a favorite game. The rewards discussed in this section are all secondary rewards.

Secondary rewards are usually distributed through reward systems. Reward systems are set up to support a specific behavior over a given period of time. For example, one youth may be given a penny each time he/she approaches an adult with a friendly smile and a handshake, while another youth may be given a point, which can be accumulated with other points to earn a trip to the video game room each time he/she goes to bed quietly. The objective is to provide something rewarding to the youth each time he/she displays a desired behavior until the behavior is internalized or repeated frequently enough to indicate to the team members that the youth will continue to display the behavior after the reward is removed.

Following are eight techniques for using reward systems:

17.1 **Emphasize the positive, not the negative, aspects of the reward system.** Statements such as, "If you don't do your homework you won't get your point," or, "If you don't stop hitting Johnnie, I will not give you your candy," are counter productive. These statements turn reward systems into takeaway systems. Statements such as "Don't forget you get a point for completing your homework," and "Try to concentrate on working together on your project so I can give you your apple" are much more effective.

17.2 **Use rewards to increase behaviors, not decrease behaviors.** It is much more positive to reward a youth for doing something as opposed to not doing something. For example, it is more positive to reward a youth for appropriately touching someone than it is to reward a youth for not putting his hands on someone else.

17.3 **Choose rewards that are meaningful to the youth.** For example, a model kit for a youth who likes to build cars, an apple for a youth who needs oral gratification, or one to one time playing catch with an adult for the sports minded youth.

17.4 **Whenever possible, choose rewards that serve several treatment purposes.** For example, building a model may increase self confidence, an apple has nutritional value, and a youth playing catch may improve his/her relationships with the adult.

17.5 **Give the reward as soon after the desired behavior as possible.** Youth who need rewards for motivation are youth who need immediate gratification. If this gratification is delayed for too long, the reward system will lose its impact very quickly.

17.6 **Keep track of the frequency of the behavior being rewarded.** Team members usually determine a reasonable frequency of occurrence for the behavior they are trying to reward. For example, the team may want the youth to comb his hair at least once a day at the beginning of a reward program and later they may expect that the youth comb his/her hair three times a day. It is important, therefore, to keep track of the frequency of the behavior in order to determine if the system is working. Usually, behavior frequencies are marked on a chart which is easily accessible to all the workers. The key to keeping accurate records is, as suggested in the reinforcement guidelines, making sure that the system is manageable.

17.7 Use charts to accentuate points earned toward bigger rewards and personal achievements. Charts, which are visible to the youth, can provide additional incentive. The charts in Figure 7 are examples of how charts can be used. Chart One was used to show a youth how he was progressing on a diet program. Notice how the downward slope is exaggerated to provide incentive. Chart Two was used to show a youth the time he was accumulating to spend listening to records alone after dinner. This was his reward for completing routine daily tasks.

Caution must be used with using visual charts. Some youths cannot tolerate visual reminders of positive growth. Team members must try to be careful not to expose these youths to more than they can handle.

17.8 Remove youths from reward systems before they leave the treatment program. When team members have determined that a youth is displaying a behavior with a desired frequency, then a system for removing the reward has to be established. This usually consists of gradually removing the reward by decreasing the number of times the youth is rewarded for the desired behavior and varying the schedule of rewards until the reward is no longer needed. In other words, the youth will display the desired behavior without a reward. While the rewarding

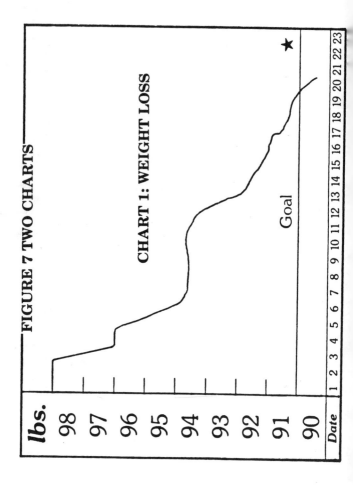

FIGURE 7 TWO CHARTS

CHART 1: WEIGHT LOSS

lbs.
98
97
96
95
94
93
92
91
90

Goal

Date 1 2 3 4 5 6 7 8 9 10 11 12 13 14 15 16 17 18 19 20 21 22 23

94

CHART TWO: TIME ACCUMULATION

Date:

	7:30- 7:45 a.m.	7:45- 8:00a.m.	8:30- 8:45 a.m.	3:00- 3:15 p.m.	accumulated time
1	OK			OK	20 min
2	OK				10 min.
3	OK	OK	OK		30 min
4	OK	OK	OK	OK	40 min
5	OK	OK		OK	30 min.
6	OK		OK	OK	30 min.
7	OK	OK	OK	OK	40 min.
8	OK	OK	OK	OK	40 min.
9	OK	OK	OK	OK	40 min.

process is being decreased, workers usually increase praise and encouragement.

18. Privilege Systems

Privileges are independent activities which youths aspire to over a given period of time. For example, a privilege may be the opportunity to go to the video parlor or store without adult supervision or time spent alone in the evening in the group living room. Privileges such as these can be very motivating to troubled youths who generally value independence more than most other incentives. However, independence is also a difficult facet of development to assess. Unlike specific behaviors which can be observed and immediately rewarded, independence emanates from a series of behaviors which are indicative of trusting relationships. For example, in order to exercise the above privileges youths would have to show their workers over a period of time that they could be trusted alone and that they had the skills needed to use the privilege. This is a much more difficult situation to assess than a reward situation such as praising a youth every time he/she washes his/her face.

Privileges are usually defined as part of a privilege system with a predetermined hierarchy of privileges. For example, a typical hierarchy begins with a very limited independence such as the right to unsupervised access to certain materials such as tools, and moves on to less limited independence such as lengthy trips into the community without adult supervision. The techniques in this section are designed to set up effective privilege systems.

Following are seven privilege techniques:

18.1 **Involve group members in establishing and reviewing the privilege hierarchy.** One of the best ways to help youths become more independent is to involve them in the decision-making process. Youths can also give the adults a better idea of what are really meaningful privileges. If the adults establish the hierarchy alone or never consult group members about revisions, the system will lose meaning for the youths.

The objectives are to establish logical privileges which match the realities in an agency's or group's social and treatment order. Consequently, no two privilege systems will be alike, because no two social or treatment situations have the same conditions to consider. Following is a simple example of a privilege system which was established for a group of youths in a residential setting. Once again, readers should pay attention to organization and not necessarily actual content.

Grooming Kit — Youth has his/her own grooming kit with various grooming supplies to keep in his/her room. Prior to obtaining the kit, adults hand out and collect materials during grooming periods.

Job Helper — Youths work with maintenance man on special jobs around the agency.

Limited Independence — Youths can play alone or unsupervised with other youths in on-grounds play areas.

Limited Off Grounds — Youths can go off grounds to a designated location such as the variety store for a limited period of time.

Off Grounds — Youths go off for extended periods of time.

Job — Youths can have jobs in the community.

18.2 **Individualize the criteria for advancement whenever possible.** Group members will have many different strengths and weaknesses related to becoming more independent. Independence is a highly individualized trait and the strength and weakness associated with obtaining independence can vary tremendously from one youth to another. Therefore, whenever possible, the criteria for advancement in the privilege system should be individualized according to the treatment plan. This can create a problem if group members are prone to comparisons, and most group members are, but it is better to struggle with their comparisons than to exclude or overlook youths whose abilities do not conform to group norms. Every youth should be recognized for his/her unique strengths.

18.3 **Explain the criteria for advancement to each youth in the group on a regular basis and check to make sure his/her perceptions are the same as the teams'.** Also check to make sure that the privileges maintain meaning or desirability for each group member.

18.4 **Emphasize the positive aspects of the privilege system.** Comments such as "That's the kind of behavior that will lead to off grounds," and "It seems to me that you are beginning to feel much more confident about being unsupervised. How do you feel?" are appropriate. Comments such as "If you don't shape up, you'll never get that privilege" only teach youth that privileges are another "club" which adults hold over their heads. Youths need to view privileges as a process that grows out of trusting relationships, not as rewards and punishments which adults take and give at their own pleasure.

18.5 **Use reward systems, praise and encouragement to help youths develop the skills needed to use a specific privilege.** For example, a reward system may be set up to teach a youth how to use the various articles in a grooming kit such as soap, toothbrush, deodorant, etc. or a youth may be praised for being courteous to a store clerk on a supervised outing.

18.6 **Always make joint assessments.** When the time comes to decide whether or not a youth is ready to use another privilege, the decision should be based on the consensus opinions of all the team members and the youth. Everyone involved must feel secure enough to allow the youth to move on. It is better to err on the side of caution than to set a youth up for failure. Once the decision to go ahead is made, the youth will have a much better chance of succeeding if everyone, including the youth, is confident that he/she can handle the privilege. Joint assessments are the only way to establish this confidence.

18.7 **Once a privilege has been obtained, treat it as a long term right and not a short term reward that can easily be taken away.** If the team is confident that a youth can handle a privilege, then team members must constantly convey the message that they respect the youth's right to his/her privilege. Comments such as "If you don't keep your room clean, I don't see why you should have off grounds," undermine the privilege system.

Summary

Troubled youths need extra assistance and support to get involved in productive growing experiences. The techniques presented in this chapter can help child/youth workers in their attempts to provide reinforcement if the guidelines at the beginning of the chapter are strongly adhered to and if workers recognize that effective reinforcement requires the same devotion to detail and awareness of individual needs as do all other direct intervention skills. Becoming an effective reinforcer is a craft that requires hours of interaction to master and a strong commitment to looking for something positive even when a youth is in an extremely negative state.

1. Driekurs, R. & Cassels, P. *Discipline without tears.* New York: Hawthorne Books, 1974, p. 55.
2. Gordon, T. *Parent Workbook.* Pasedena, California: Effectiveness Training Association, 1972, p. 5.
3. Ginot, H. *Between parent and child.* New York: McMillan, 1965, p. 39.
4. Driekurs, op. cit., p. 49.
5. Mayer, M. *A guide for child care workers.* New York: Child Welfare league of America, 1958, p. 28.

CHAPTER FIVE

DISCIPLINE ALTERNATIVES TO PUNISHMENT

Discipline alternatives are the positive methods of procedure or practices which child/youth workers use to control or correct inappropriate behavior. The title discipline alternatives to punishment was chosen because I believe there is sufficient evidence to indicate that punishment, one form of discipline, is not an effective technique to use with troubled youth. Punishment may provide immediate control in some situations, but over the long run it usually leads to more severe behavior patterns than the ones the user was trying to correct.[1] In other words, punishment reinforces youths' poor self images and this often leads to more self distructive behavior. Discipline alternatives, on the other hand, can be effective if used as part of an overall positive approach or treatment plan. Effective discipline alternatives improve youths' self images and lead to more self fulfilling behavior.

Following are descriptions of the characteristics I believe differentiate an effective discipline alternative from punishment (see Figure 8):

Prevention — Before a discipline alternative is used, all of the preventive alternatives are exhausted first. This means that child/youth workers look at their relationships, the treatment environment and specific activities to see if there is anything which can be changed to prevent the youth from acting inappropriately. Once all the

Figure 8
A Comparison of Alternatives and Punishment

Discipline Alternatives

1. Emphasis on preventing the problem before it occurs.

2. Consequences are discussed together by adults and youth (whenever possible in advance of the problem).

3. Emphasis is on teaching reality of the social order.

4. Requires internal control.

5. Psychological and physical pain are not o.k.

6. Reinvolvement is a priority.

Punishment

1. Emphasis on dealing with problem after it occurs.

2. Consequences are set by adults (usually following the problem).

3. Emphasis on the reality of adult authority.

4. Relies on external control.

5. Psychological and physical are o.k.

6. Exclusion is a priority.

possible changes are made or proposed then the alternative is chosen in case the behavior still persists after the prevention strategies are employed.

Punishment focuses entirely on dealing with a problem after it occurs. It relies on the penalty or pain which is suffered after behaving inappropriately to deter the offender from behaving the same way in the future.

Consequences — Effective discipline alternatives concentrate on setting logical consequences together with the youth(s) beforehand. The objectives are to reach a mutual agreement about what will happen if the youth decides to misbehave and to avoid power struggles when the youth is misbehaving by being able to refer back to the mutual agreement. For example, a group may decide beforehand that the consequence for goofing around in the group van is to pull over to the side of the road and wait until everyone is settled and then return to the agency rather than proceeding to the designated activity.

Punishment relies on consequences which are frequently introduced for the first time after a behavior occurs. For example, the worker may stop the van and tell all the group members that he/she is returning to the agency where everyone will spend an hour in his/her room for not behaving in the van. These situations tend to increase power struggles and to create confusion abut the relationship between the penalty and the offense.

Reality of the Social Order — Discipline

alternatives are based on consequences which reflect the reality of the social order. In other words, the consequences which are derived together are logically related to the social conditions which prevail among group members. For example, a group may decide that the consequence for being late to breakfast is to be awakened earlier. In this particular setting, missing breakfast is not an option nor is it fair for the worker to spend time with one youth who is lagging behind the group. Thus, the logical consequence reflects the social needs of all group members.

Punishment reflects the reality of the adults' authority. For example, the adult tells the youth who is late for breakfast that he will have to work for an hour after school because the adult said so. This approach creates two major problems. First, youths learn very little about their own authority when adults constantly impose their authority on them. They continue to perceive adults as being in total control of their lives. Second, youths today are much more likely to ask why or engage in power struggles than youths in the past. Youths have been exposed through the media to adults disagreeing about many major issues. For example, they frequently see their sports heroes arguing with each other and officials, and they witness politicians debating different sides of an issue. Consequently, they do not believe that there is a consensus adult authority or opinion and they are much more likely to challenge adults who rely totally on authority.

Internal Control — Discipline alternatives teach youths that they have the internal control to regain their composure. For example, an adult reminds a youth that he must leave the activity until he is able to show that he can return. Or, the consequence for not cleaning one's room is that the youth is responsible for cleaning the room before moving on to the next activity.

Punishment relies on external control. For example, the adult tells a youth that he/she must leave the activity until the adult is ready to allow the youth to return. Or, a youth is placed in a locked confinement room for fifteen minutes.

Psychological and Physical Pain are Not O.K. — Discipline alternatives assume that psychological and physical pain are not O.K. Youths are in a state of ego deterioration when they are misbehaving and more pain enhances, not relieves, ego deterioration.[2] For example, deprivation of food, sleep, and clothing; belittling remarks; or physically painful intervention such as sitting or arm twisting only serve to further convince troubled youths that they are no good.

Punishment assumes that more psychological and physical pain will reduce undesirable behavior patterns. The problem with this line of thinking is that most troubled youths have experienced an abnormal amount of psychological and physical pain prior to entering youth care programs. If this technique worked, they would be the healthiest youths in the world.

Reinvolvement a Priority — Discipline alternatives encourage youths to return to the ongoing activity as soon as possible. Since ongoing activities are considered to be part of the treatment process, the objective is to include youths in as much of this process as possible. Therefore, the message with an effective discipline alternative is always "we want you back as soon as you are ready to return."

Punishment emphasizes exclusion. The message is "you are no good, so we don't want you as part of our group."

Whenever child/youth workers are attempting to use a discipline alternative, the outcome will be much more positive if most of the characteristics of a productive discipline alternative just presented are part of their criteria for selecting a technique. The discipline alternative techniques in this chapter provide examples of how these characteristics can be integrated into interventions. The techniques are titled:

1. Group Consequences
2. Individual Consequences
3. Time Outs
4. Restrictions
5. Physical Restraints

Discipline Alternative Guidelines

The following guidelines can be applied to using all of the discipline alternative techniques presented in this chapter:

1. Once again, the diagnostic and target behavior sections of the treatment plan should be used to set realistic expectations and to identify specific behaviors.

Discipline alternatives are effective when expectations are realistic and behaviors are specific. For example, it is difficult if not impossible to expect a youth who swears constantly to suddenly stop all of his swearing. It may be much more practical to begin by focusing on just one situation or period during the day when swearing creates the greatest problem for the youth and then move on to other situations and time periods. It is also harder to correct a diffuse behavior such as inappropriate touching than it is to correct a specific behavior such as tapping or punching fellow group members on the shoulder during breakfast.

2. Discipline alternatives will work best with authoritative relationships.

An authoritative child/youth worker assumes ultimate responsiblity for a youth's security and safety, but in a rational issue-oriented manner. Such a worker values self-will and autonomy. Verbal give and take are encouraged, and the child/youth worker attempts to exercise his/her authority by frequent explanations of his/her reasons for demands or prohibitions. In authoritative relationships, youths participate and contribute to discussions of issues relevant to their behavior and frequently take part in establishing consequences; however, the adult does not abdicate ultimate responsibility. [2]

3. A few superordinate rules are needed to enhance the effectiveness of individualized discipline alternatives.

Superordinate rules are rules which every member of a program can agree upon. For example, a program may have rules for major issues such as use of drugs, stealing or physically harming a person. These are superordinate rules if all the members of the organization can support and enforce the consequences, and express confidence in the reasoning behind the rules. Troubled youths need to know that there are a few rules which adults can agree on and which are consistent with the values and beliefs of all individual staff members. It is much easier for a youth to respond to individualized consequences and for an adult to enforce consequences, if the youth and the adults are aware that all the adults can work together on major issues which are of vital concern to everyone.

4. **Consequences must be manageable for all the team members who are expected to participate in using a specific discipline alternative.**

The discipline alternative consequences must be enforceable and the youths' behavior observable or the alternatives cannot possibly work. The same precautions that are taken with reinforcement techniques should also be taken in matching a discipline alternative to a specific treatment environment (see guideline 4. Chapter Four).

19. Group Consequences

Group consequences are based on a group's ability to set logical consequences for inappropriate behavior together prior to the occurrence of identified behaviors. The objectives are for the group to come to mutual agreement about a relevant solution for handling a problem before it occurs, and to place the adult in a position where he/she can say, "Remember, we talked about this together," when the problem occurs. This reduces the potential for a power struggle, generates group support and creates a logical connection between the behavior and the consequence. For example, a group of youths and their child/youth workers may determine that the consequences for breaking an item of furniture in the group living or meeting room is to have the offender pay for the furniture or part of the furniture out of his/her own resources. Then, when an incident occurs, the workers merely remind the youth of the preestablished consequence.

Group consequences can only be used when the behavior which creates problems for the group is a behavior that is common to all the group's members. Group consequences are not intended to single out or identify an individual group member. This technique should not be confused with group techniques which are designed to generate negative peer pressure toward one member of a group. I feel these techniques are generally ineffective and if attempted at all, should only be attempted in highly controlled environments. Techniques for individual behavior problems will be discussed in following sections.

Following are five group consequence techniques:

19.1 **Identify the behavior problem which is common to all the group members.** For example, grabbing food at the table, stalling before activities, starting fights during transitions, disruptive play in a moving vehicle, and being late for showers are the types of behaviors which can be common to

110

most of the members in a given group of youths. These constitute behavior that disrupt group functioning, but not necessarily the type of behavior which requires highly individualized attention.

19.2 **Facilitate a discussion among group members to determine a logical consequence for the chosen behavior.** The discussion begins by making sure that all group members recognize the problem and proceeds by exploring alternative courses of action. The adults' role as facilitator varies from group to group with younger children generally needing more guidance and older youths less guidance. The following example summarizes a group discussion about consequences.

Group Leader: "Hey guys, we have a problem I'd like to discuss with the whole group. You know from time to time one group member or another will stall or goof around right when we're supposed to go off to the recreation room. Then I have to spend time trying to get one or two guys going and the rest of the group has to wait. The end result is usually that we miss part of our time the rec room. How can we solve this problem? First, let me ask this question. Is there something about the activities in the rec room that makes any of you want to avoid the activity?"

Group Member: "Yeah, you expect us to do too many exercises before we start to play

111

the games."

Group Leader: "O.K. I'm willing to take a look at that. Maybe I can reduce the number of exercises we're doing. Now, what do you think we should do if the problem continues even after the exercises are reduced?"

Group Member: "Take away all their privileges and keep them in their room all day."

Group Leader: "No, no; remember, we decided that group activities are required and it's much better if we all participate together."

Group Member: "Have him make up the activity. If he won't come and he tries to get all your attention, you should leave him behind and come with the rest of us."

Group Leader: "How can we do that without taking time away from the group later?"

Group Member: "During free time you can get him and have him make up the activity with some guys from the other groups. The rest of us can be on our own like the other guys who are behaving. Anybody who's messing around during group activities shouldn't be left alone during free time anyways."

Group Leader: "How does that sound to the rest of you?"

Group Members: "Yeah; okay."

Group Leader: "Okay, the next time it happens I'm only going to remind the guy once. If he doesn't come, I won't say anything until free period. But remember, we would really prefer to have everyone participate together the first time."

19.3 **Cover as many of the discipline alternative characteristics defined at the beginning of the chapter in the discussion as possible.** For example, in the previous example, (a) preventive alternatives were explored first, (b) the consequence was discussed together beforehand, (c) the final consequence reflected the social order for this group, (d) and internal control and reinvolvement were emphasized.

19.4 **When an agreement is reached, tell the group members that the consequence will have to be approved by the total treatment team.** Then seek approval before using the consequence.

19.5 **Practice group discussions about consequences as frequently as possible.** Don't expect to be an effective group facilitator overnight. The group consequence process requires practice and patience, as do most effective discipline alternatives.

20. Individual Consequences

Individual consequences are similar to group consequences. The major difference is that consequences are set by the adult and one youth as opposed to all the group members. The objective is to establish a logical consequence ahead of time for a behavior problem which is causing special problems for a youth. In this context, individual consequences can be used with most of the inappropriate or circular effect behaviors identified in the individual treatment plan.

Following are six individual consequence techniques:

20.1 **Discuss problem behaviors together as a team, before holding individual discussions with individual youth.** Team members should agree that the behavior is a problem and that they are willing to use individual consequences. Then a team member or team members should be designated to hold a discussion with the youth.

20.2 **Begin the discussion with the youth by identifying the behavior problem together.** The task is to make sure that both parties clearly recognize the behavior as a problem. If the youth does not agree, further discussions may be required.

20.3 **Facilitate the discussion by exploring various preventive and corrective alternatives, and try to steer the discussion toward an effective discipline alternative, as defined earlier.**

20.4 **Choose a consequence which meets the youth's treatment and social needs.** It is impossible to provide a list of effective consequences because consequences must be individualized and a consequence which is effective for one youth may be totally inappropriate for another. The following list is presented merely to give you an idea of some of the consequences I used in my practice:

1. Making-up activities.
2. Cleaning up a mess before moving on to the next activity.
3. Returning from trips when the group acted up in a vehicle.
4. Paying a prorated fee for broken items.
5. Short restrictions (see 22 Restrictions).
6. Time-outs (see 21. Time-Outs)

Generally, an attempt should be made to avoid consequences which may give negative connotations to a desired behavior. For example, if a team is trying to get a youth to develop work or writing skills, then work hours and writing papers should not be consequences for inappropriate behavior. When this happens youths begin to associate a desired skill with doing something undesirable.

20.5 **When an agreement is reached, explain to the youth that the rest of the treatment team will have to approve the consequence.** A consensus agreement is needed among team members in order to effectively implement the consequence. Once the consequence is approved, it becomes an additional part of the youth's treatment plan.

20.6 **Assess the effectiveness of a consequence by the frequency with which it used.** An effective consequence should give desired results in a relatively short period of time. When a consequence must be used repeatedly, it is time to look at an alternative strategy.

21. Time Outs

Time outs and the remaining discipline alternatives in this chapter are discipline alternatives which should be used as a last resort after all of the previous alternatives presented in this book have been exhausted. Under favorable conditions, these techniques should be the results of group and individual consequence discussions. Under less favorable conditions, child/youth workers will have to use these techniques without prior discussion with youth.

A time out is a brief period of isolation from the on-going activity. For example, a youth who is disrupting a group discussion by making loud and obnoxious noises may be requested to leave the room until he/she is ready to participate in the discussion. Or, a youth who is running wildly around the group game room may be asked to take a short time out to settle down.

The amount of time the youth remains away from the activity can be approached in two ways. First, most behaviorists or advocates of behavior modification believe that short time outs of approximately five minutes are most effective. In other words, a worker using this approach tells the youth that he/she will have to leave the activity for five minutes.

Another school of thought suggests that it is better to convey the message that the youth can return as soon as he/she is ready to participate. In other words, a worker using this approach tells the youth to leave the activity until he/she is ready to return.

I favor the latter approach for three reasons. First, the emphasis with this approach is on having the youth return as soon as he/she is ready and not when the time runs out. This means that internal and not external control determines when a youth returns and it conveys the message that the youth is wanted back as soon as possible. Second, troubled youths often lose their time concept when they are anxious. Hence, a reasonable five-minute time out may seem like all day to an upset youth. It is not unusual for a worker to respond to a youth who is not cooperating in taking a five minute timeout by saying "O.K. that's fifteen minutes" or "You owe me another ten minutes later on." And if the youth doesn't respond, the struggle and the time may escalate even further.

There is no question that the open-ended approach takes considerable practice and a thorough knowledge of the youth's ability to recuperate, but I am convinced after several years of struggling with the time fixing method that over the long run the open-ended approach is better. Therefore, child/ youth care workers are encouraged to try this approach whenever possible.

Following are six techniques which will help with open-ended time outs. These techniques can also be applied to the time fixing approach by those workers who are not sold on the open-ended method.

21.1 **Whenever possible, explore the possibilities of making a time out a group or individual consequence.** That is, if other alternatives have been exhausted, it is better to have a mutual agreement beforehand to use time outs than to not have an agreement. Following is an example of a discussion about using a time out as an individual consequence.

Worker: "John, the team was reviewing your treatment plan the other day and we noticed that you were still having trouble with teasing other group members during group discussions. For example, the other night you started calling Ron and Bill names in the middle of our discussion about Christmas vacation. Do you remember?"

John: "Yeah, I remember."

Worker: "Can you see how this causes problems?"

John: "Yeah, I guess so. But sometimes I don't like talking about the things we talk about."

Worker: "Oh, what is it you don't like?"

John: "Well, some of those things really make me feel bad."

Worker: "You mean our discussions make you think about unpleasant things."

John: "Yeah, I remember stuff that happened when I was at home."

Worker: "O.K., I'll tell you what. In the future, I'll let you know ahead of time, whenever I can, what we are going to talk about. Then, if you are worried, we can talk about it beforehand. Is that fair?"

John: "It sounds O.K."

Worker: "Now, if you still tease at meetings, what should we do?"

John: "Kick me out of the meeting."

Worker: "Well, we really want you at those meetings. That's when we make all kinds of decisions about consequences and plan activities. You should be part of the decision-making process."

John: "You're right. Besides I like to make some of the decisions.

Worker: "How about if we ask you to leave until you are ready to return?"

John: "You mean I can come back as soon as I show you I'm ready?"

Worker: "Yes."

John: "What if I think I'm ready and you don't?"

Worker: "That's something we'll have to work at together. I want to talk to you about that next, but first, do we agree on the consequence for teasing?"

John: "O.K., let's try it."

Worker: "All right, now let's talk about the kind of behavior it will take to come back to the group."

21.2 **Hold team discussions to determine a youth's ability to recuperate.** Team members can help each other determine what can be expected when a youth is asked to leave an activity until he/she is ready to return. How long does it take for the youth to settle down and is the youth likely to return before he/she is really settled, are the kinds of questions that team members can explore together.

21.3 **When the time out is being administered, remain as calm as possible.** If you are out of control or convey a negative attitude the time out will turn into a punishment or power struggle and make the youth feel worse than he/she already feels. For example, the worker who shouts, "Get the hell out of here and don't return until you are ready," is defeating the purpose of the time out which is to help the youth reintegrate as soon as possible. A more appropriate comment is "Bill, I'd like you to leave the activity until you feel you can return and join us in a more productive way. We want you back as soon as possible. I'm sure if you give it a little thought, you'll be ready in a few moments."

21.4 Designate a time out area which is as close to the activity as possible. This is a judgment call. The objective is to have the youth nearby so he/she feels the group really wants him/her back, but to make sure that the youth is in a location that is not too stimulating to the group or the youth. You don't want to start behavior contagion or allow the group to apply negative peer pressure, but you do want the youth to have easy access to the activity.

21.5 Designate a time out area which is comfortable and non-threatening. Time outs become punishment when the youths are frightened or placed in physically uncomfortable positions or locations. A good time out location is a place where the youth can concentrate on "getting it back together" or restoring ego strength without being concerned about negative environmental stimuli.

21.6 Make sure that the youth is really ready before permitting a return to the activity. This is perhaps the most difficult part of an effective time out, because it requires a good knowledge of the youth and his/her ability to reintegrate or be ready to behave once again in a more self productive way. But then, most effective intervention techniques require a good knowlege of the youth. If a youth continues to return to activity "out of shape" or in a continued state of ego deterioration, then another technique should be considered. Time outs are only effective when a youth truly does have the ability and wants to return to the on-going activity.

22. Restrictions

Restrictions are temporary restraints on rights of access to desirable experiences. For example, a restriction is usually the consequence for abusing one of the privileges in a privilege system (a youth may be restricted from using T.V. which he/she previously handled in a rough manner). The key word in the above definition is temporary, because generally youth are being restricted from experiences which have a positive treatment value and therefore, the objective is to restore the right to access as soon as possible. Restrictions are also most effective when used on an infrequent basis. If a restriction is used too frequently, then it is the privilege or the youth's ability to use the privilege which is the problem and further restrictions will only increase, not decrease, the problem.

Following are five restriction techniques:

22.1 **Whenever possible use 19. Group Consequence and 20. Individual Consequence techniques to establish a restriction as a consequence.** For example, the group may determine that a logical consequence for returning late from an off grounds or community trip is a one-day restriction. Or, a youth may agree that the logical consequence for leaving a mess in the group meeting room is to clean the room during free play time.

22.2 **Keep restrictions as short as possible.** If a youth is really capable of using a privilege or being involved in some other growth producing experience, then short restrictions will be very effective. For example, if a fairly trustworthy youth is late from a trip to the community, then a brief one-day restriction should be effective. On the other hand, if a youth steals cigarettes from a drugstore, a short restriction will not be beneficial because the youth was probably not ready to handle the experience in the first place.

22.3 **Avoid using restrictions as threats.** Any time you use a discipline alternative as a threat, it loses its effectiveness. With restrictions, this is a special problem because restrictions are usually connected with privileges and when adults are constantly threatening to take away privileges, youths quickly get the message that they cannot be independent (see 18. Privileges). One calm reminder that if the behavior continues, a restriction will be necessary, should be sufficient in most cases.

22.4 **Make sure the restriction is related to the privilege or growing experience which has been abused.** For example a short restriction from using the television room alone is effective for youths who were caught wrestling while alone in the room, but not for youths who forget to clean their rooms or fail to finish their homework. In the latter cases, it is more effective to set consequences which suggest that these tasks must be completed before they can use the T.V. room rather than threaten a restriction.

22.5 **Use restriction frequencies as barometers for assessing effectiveness.** Restrictions, like other consequences, are effective on an infrequent basis. If a restriction is needed repeatedly, then the treatment team must reassess the problem or level of independence a youth has been given.

23. Physical Control Techniques

When youths lose self control to the point where they are about to harm themselves or others, or destroy valuable property, then workers must use their own physical strength to control the youth. Physical controls are the procedures child/youth workers use to physically hold youth without harming them. The objective is to provide secure physical control until the youth can regain his/her control. This is not an easy task, but with the proper attitudes and support, physical control can be an effective method of intervention.

I found that the following conditions were usually present when physical control turned out to be a positive experience for youth.

1. The child/youth worker who could provide positive physical control was not necessarily a worker who was physically strong, but a worker who could take charge of the situation. For example, a 5'1" woman who could call for help and direct her fellow workers to get a youth under control was just as effective as a larger worker who could do it by himself/herself. In other words, the important factor was ability to take charge, not size.

2. All the workers in the program were willing to help each other. When child/youth workers had to work in isolation or without adequate support, it was almost impossible to use appropriate physical control. On the other hand, if the youths knew that there was adequate support and a willingness among workers to help out, then physical control was minimized and when it was used, it turned out to be more productive for everyone involved.

3. The child/youth care workers felt secure enough about themselves that they did not need to engage in physical confrontation, or win power struggles to show the youths they were in charge. When youths sensed that physical control and power struggles were major issues with the adults, the tendency was to test the adult's authority. On the other hand, when youths sensed that adults did not need to physically confront or win power struggles in order to feel secure about themselves, they tended not to test these issues.

Following are nine physical control techniques:

23.1 Be conscious of the factors that enhance the probability that the youth

will lose control and do everything possible to eliminate these factors. Physical control techniques are the last set of techniques in this book for a good reason; child/youth workers now have at least 22 sets of techniques which can be used before physical control.

23.2 **Hold team discussions to determine what constitutes the need for physical control with a specific youth and clearly define limits for using physical control in the youth's treatment plan.** The capacity to lose control, or intensity of temper tantrums varies tremendously from one youth to another. Therefore, team members must be as certain as possible that physical control is the correct answer.

23.3 **Once a determination has been made that a youth must be held, approach the youth as cautiously as possible.** Take every precaution possible to protect yourself. If the youth is too large or strong, seek additional help before intervening. Also, avoid wearing objects which can be easily grabbed or pulled on.

23.4 **Unless it is physically impossible or totally unsafe, remove the youth from the seeing and hearing range of others.** One method is to walk the youth backwards while holding his/her arms folded across the chest. Never pull a youth by one of his/her limbs or bend a limb in a direction opposite to its intended direction.

23.5 **When an appropriate location is found, hold the youth in as secure and painless a posture as possible.** One method is to lay the youth on his/her stomach on a soft spot such as a bed or fluffy rug while holding his/her arms folded under the chest or chin, but not the neck. Sit on the youth's buttocks to avoid placing excess weight on his/her stomach and place your feet across the youth's inner knee to avoid being kicked. When two adults are available have one adult hold the feet.

Another method involves holding a youth between your legs while sitting on the floor with your back against a comfortable nonmovable object. Then cross the youth's arms across his chest and sit behind him/her making sure that he/she cannot hit you with his/her head. It is also helpful to wrap your legs over the top of the youth's legs to keep him/her from kicking and squirming. This approach works best with smaller youths.

These methods may or may not be appropriate for your setting. Therefore, you are encouraged to be aware of specific holding techniques which are used at your agency. If the techniques at your agency are questionable, please do not use the techniques without outside consultation from a reliable source.

23.6 **Sit quietly until the youth is ready to listen to you· talk in a calm voice.** This is not the time to win arguments or to shout. Nor is it the time to discuss feelings or respond to inappropriate comments.

23.7 **Once the youth appears to be ready, begin to calmly talk about how you will release the hold.** For example, say: "When I feel you are ready, I'm going to release one arm, then the next." When this has been accomplished then give the next instruction, "Next I'll release your feet and then I want you to go over and sit quietly on that chair." Never proceed from one step to the next unless you are reasonably sure that the youth has sufficient control.

23.8 **After the youth has regained control and is sitting quietly in the designated area, ask if he/she would like to be alone for a few moments.** Both of you are likely to be exhausted.

23.9 **Choose an appropriate time, not too long after the youth has settled down, to talk with him/her about the incident.** Some workers prefer to talk to a youth about the incident while he/she is still being held, but in my practice it always seemed best to wait until both parties had a chance to completely settle down. Use your own judgment to determine which will work best for the youths in your program. At the end of a discussion always point out more productive alternatives.

Locked Confinement

Locked confinement is the practice of locking in an isolation room youths who are acting out or physically out of control. Locked confinement techniques will not be presented in this chapter, because I believe that locked confinement is an extremely punitive practice. The reason the topic is brought up is because I hope that child/youth workers who read this book and work in agencies using locked confinement are now more aware of productive alternatives and understand that locked confinement has all of the characteristics of a non-productive punishment presented at the beginning of the chapter.

When a situation reaches a point where locked confinement is normally used, it is recommended that time out or physical control techniques be used instead. If this requires, "timing a youth out" or controlling a youth in an isolated room, then the door should be unlocked and if necessary the adult should be in the room with the youth.

Summary

This chapter is the last technique chapter because discipline alternatives, as defined earlier, should be used after all the other techniques in the previous chapters have been exhausted. When workers reach the point where discipline is needed, the characteristics and guidelines presented at the beginning of the chapter should be foremost in their minds. In other words, discipline alternatives can be effective, but only when the proper precautions are taken and when discipline is placed last in terms of treatment priorities.

1. Bergin, A., & Garfield, S. *Handbook of psychotherapy and behavior change.* New York John Wiley and Sons, 1971, p. 583.

2. Conger, J. *Adolescence and youth: Psychological development in a changing world.* New York: Harper and Row, 1979, p. 200.

3. Driekurs, R. & Cassels, P. *Discipline without tears.* New York: Hawthorne Books, 1974.

CHAPTER SIX

SELF-CARE PROGRAMS

In the final two chapters, several examples will be presented to show how intevention techniques can be integrated into comprehensive treatment programs. Treatment programs are systematic approaches to treating major developmental strengths and weaknesses. Treatment programs do not replace treatment plans, but serve instead to concentrate several intervention techniques on one or more of the needs identified in treatment plans. In this context, a treatment program can be an individual or group program depending on the commonality of the need or behavior being addressed. For example, a group grooming program would be developed if more than one member of a group needed help with grooming skills, but if only one member needed help, then an individual program would be developed. Once a program is developed, it becomes an additional part of the treatment strategy for all the youths involved in the program.

All of the remaining examples are programs which were designed and implemented by child/youth workers. In each instance, the workers were part of a treatment team and they based their programs on the individual needs of the youths in their group. Many of the intervention techniques these workers integrated into their programs were the same as the intervention techniques presented previously. However, several additional techniques were also designed by the workers to address specific problems.

The programs in this chapter were prepared to develop basic self-care skills such as eating, grooming and health care. Self-care programs play a significant role in treating troubled youth, because treatment usually begins with something simple or concrete such as learning to make one's bed or shampooing one's hair and then moves on to more complex social and emotional issues. In other words, it is easier for troubled youths to tackle more difficult, less concrete tasks, if they have developed the self-confidence which comes from being able to master basic self care tasks. Thus, self-care programs usually have two purposes. The first is to teach basic self-care skills and the second is to act as a catalyst for growth in other related areas. The self-care programs chosen for this chapter served both of these purposes. The program titles are:

1. A Diet Program
2. An Enuresis Program
3. Two Mealtime Programs
4. Two Grooming Programs
5. A Medication Program

A Diet Program

The first program is a diet program designed for three overweight emotionally disturbed boys by three child/youth workers. The workers used recording and observing techniques to develop and monitor the program and a variety of activity, reinforcement, and discipline alternatives to punishment techniques to implement the program.

Background Information

Up until the program began, the workers had

been hesitant to attempt anything that involved food deprivation because of the possible emotional or social consequences. They felt that the security and pleasure a youth received from proper food intake was something they could not afford to take away from someone who had already been deprived of too much. It was their hope that diet and physical appearance would improve along with emotional growth. Unfortunately, this did not prove to be true. All three boys remained overweight. Emotional growth lagged as the boys filled the image their physical condition conveyed. In others words, they used being overweight as a means of gaining attention. They knew that encouraging their participation in activities took an extra effort on the part of the workers. Furthermore, the problem was usually compounded even more by the fact that once these youths were involved, they usually failed. This created negative circular effects that were very difficult to break through.

Since all three boys had been at the center over a year, the workers felt a new approach was needed. They believed there was now an element of trust in their relationships and that this trust would make it easier for the youths to accept food deprivation. Their new position was that emotional and cognitive growth would be related to weight loss. As the youths' physical self-concept improved, so would their abilities to cope with feelings and interact with others. This would create positive circular effects, making it possible for adults and peers to socially reinforce rather than reject the boys. The following program was developed to see if this concept was accurate or not:

The Program

These three youths were all in the same group of seven. This meant they handled daily routines together, participated in group activities together and ate together. All three had gained weight prior to starting the program.

Diet: The actual diet was based on recommendations of the center's doctor. He had treated the three youths since their arrival and was qualified to make a decision that would not endanger their health. A one thousand calorie diet was decided upon as the safest way to reach the program's goal of average weight based on height for one's age. The one thousand calories were proportioned among three meals and no exceptions were allowed. After a brief time, however, the doctor was consulted and six ounces of diet soda were permitted at bedtime. The workers weighed the youths each morning, and their weights were charted. The object was to enable the youths to see progress on a daily basis. All staff were informed of the program and instructed not to convey any negative feelings regarding overweight. Praise was used as reinforcement for weight loss, as it was for all aspects of the program.

Diet proved to be the most successful part of the program, belying others' doubts, advice from more experienced persons and the difficulties of institutional eating processes. All three lost more than twenty five pounds.

Appearance: A special effort was made each day to make sure that the youths tried to look the best they could. This included good personal hygiene, proper dress and a general feeling of pride in their appearance. As the youths lost weight, new clothes were purchased.

The change in appearance, due to weight loss, acted as a catalyst and their efforts to care for themselves increased. The ability to see one's self in a better physical light served as a better motivator than any factors emphasized previously.

Group Participation: The youths were encouraged to become involved in all group activities, the premise being that the activities should be kept at a simple enough level so that each boy could see success. In many instances, this meant tailoring otherwise competitive games or complex craft projects down to a simple hour of teaching fundamentals. They were then gradually introduced into more challenging activity.

Once again, weight loss seemed to act as a catalyst. The youths learned to try new things, and as a result, learned new skills. These skills gave them something with which to occupy time previously spent trying to find something to eat or lying on their beds trying to avoid the group.

Physical Education: This was a simple part of

the program based on participation rather than on achievement of specific goals. The boys were required to get up each day and exercise before breakfast. Emphasis was placed on individual improvement and not on attainment of the norm.

In this area, each boy progressed substantially. The absence of burdensome weight made athletic accomplishments easier. The amount of exercise, running ability and basic athletic skill all increased. Consequently, the boys soon became eager to spend their free time playing group games instead of being frightened away by feelings of inadequacy.

Responsibility to Continue: Responsibility to continue meant the ability to adhere to the program while absent from supervision. It could also be interpreted as the program's tendency to instill its basic objective — wanting to maintain physical appearance. This was the most controversial aspect of the program. Responsibility was not as easily measured as a change in appearance or increased physical abilities. What's more, it could not be as directly related to the program, because it took place only in the absence of external program controls. Finally, it was almost impossible to determine whether the program was instilling the necessary desire to be responsible or if this was a result of some outside factor.

As a check, each boy was weighed prior to and immediately after returning from a home visit. In the later stages of the program, the same procedure was followed with eating lunches at school. Other

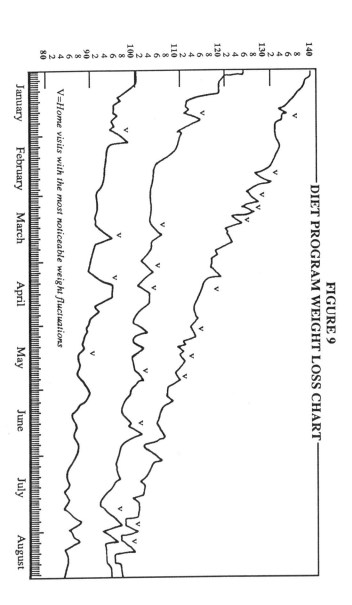

FIGURE 9
DIET PROGRAM WEIGHT LOSS CHART

V=Home visits with the most noticeable weight fluctuations

January   February   March   April   May   June   July   August

assessments were based on information shared by teachers and parents plus the workers' analyses of behavior following home visits.

The evaluation process included determining "successful visits" which were based on the lack of weight gain and continuation of positive behavior patterns after home visits. Observations were recorded in daily logs for several days after each visit. As depicted in Figure 9, successful visits were most numerous in the middle stages of the program and most lacking at the onset and toward the final discharge.

Success during the middle stages was attributed to a gradual acceptance of the program by the youths and their parents. This also was the period when the program began to gain momentum and progress in all areas was strongly supported by all staff.

The failure at the onset was contributed to the newness of the program to the youths and to the parents lack of awareness of what was being attempted. The failure near discharge is more difficult to explain. The most rational explanation probably centers around the parents' apprehension about accepting youths whose self-image and physical appearance were improving at a faster rate than the other family members. This forced the youths to resort to old forms of behavior to get parental attention.

Case History

At the onset of the program, Jim was faced with many personal problems. He was about forty-five pounds overweight, and he was preoccupied by many fears that he acted out through numerous worlds of fantasy. The most common of these was the "World of Oz." He talked continually, and used this as a defense against adult attempts to reason with him. He disliked group activities and participated only with constant adult support and encouragement. His physical condition prohibited him from mastering most average athletic skills, and when he tried, failure was likely. This caused one child care worker to comment, "I can't even take our group on a bike trip. Jim will go only a short way, and then he gets too tired to go on."

In school Jim was several grades behind the appropriate age level in all subjects. During the program he moved from the center's classroom to a special class in the community. This class consisted of children from the center, but while at school he also had a chance to communicate with community children. Although he advanced his grade during the program, he still did not reach the appropriate age grade level.

Jim's family situation was similar to that of many disturbed boys. He had been placed in a foster home for a time and then returned to his family. His mother and father had trouble communicating with each other, and his father was very passive, leaving the mother to handle most of the discipline. This was worked on throughout the program by the social worker and eventually the father began to show signs of increased involvement with Jim. Jim's mother and sister also had weight problems. Hence, family therapy concentrated on trying to help them deal with their feelings about Jim accomplishing something they weren't able to accomplish.

After seven months, Jim had lost forty five pounds and was close to average weight for his height and age. Times previously spent lying on his bed day-dreaming were now filled with active group games. Although he still talked excessively, his conversation became more positive and achievement oriented. Jim eagerly awaited group periods and at times he was almost overly excited in anticipation of an up-coming activity. The boys in the group grew to like him and a group sociogram confirmed this. Previously he got tired walking a few blocks, now he could run almost a half a mile. These new attributes also gave him a totally new image which adults found much easier to respond to with positive reinforcement.

Summary

This program was chosen as the opening example, because several techniques were successfully integrated into a comprehensive program which addressed the self care needs of three youths in a specific group. Weight loss is also a tangible measure of growth which can be related to or associated with other measures of growth. This is not always the case with self care programs, but the basic objective is usually the same: workers identify needs in individual treatment plans and then proceed to help youth develop the self caring skills or strengths which are likely to serve as catalysts to growth in other areas.

An Enuresis Program

This program was designed for an enuretic (bedwetting) youth by a worker who recognized that the youth would have to be free of ridicule and labeling that surrounded this problem before he could make significant progress within the group setting.[1] The program represents another comprehensive example of what innovative and creative workers can accomplish.

Background Information

Several significant elements stand out in this case. The coincidence of the onset of the symptom with a severe emotional trauma (separation from his mother) and the history of prior emotional disturbances indicated strong psychological foundations for Mike's enuresis. The absence of physical abnormalities confirmed this assessment. Mike's psychological profile revealed strong feelings of abandonment, rage, guilt and helplessness. The team saw Mike as an extremely anxious youth with many past and present unmet dependency needs. The persistent nocturnal enuresis was seen as an unconsious symptom of the high level of internalized anxiety stemming from past events. The feelings were maintained by daily conflicts and pressures encountered in the treatment environment and the continual presence of his feelings of abandonment and insecurity.

It was felt that the reduction of Mike's anxiety level would have a direct bearing on the frequency of his bedwetting. The issue of separation would be the most difficult one to approach. It was highly unlikely, either then or in the near future, that Mike would possess the emotional fortitude to satisfactorily resolve or understand the dynamics that led to the separation from his natural mother. The approach in this area was designed to deintensify those feelings which resulted from the separation, rather than to concentrate on helping Mike to understand what happened or why. In other words, removal from the home left many emotional "voids" which had to be filled.

The Program

The following areas were designed and implemented to reduce Mike's anxiety level and meet his daily emotional needs. The approach combines mechanical, as well as "psychological" adjustments to achieve these goals.

Mechanical: The following measures were implemented after the team obtained Mike's approval and cooperation. They were presented to him as suggestions which the adults felt would be helpful in fulfilling his desire to curb his bedwetting. Compliance was left up to Mike, and the team did not pressure him in any way.

1. Restriction of fluids during the evening. If liquid refreshments were included in the customary evening snack, an alternative such as fruit or cookies was provided.

2. Wearing pajamas at bedtime. New pajamas were supplied to Mike and he was encouraged to use them. This was done primarily to insure that he would be warm and comfortable through the night, and help

him feel good about bedtime.

3. Environmental adjustments. Precautions were taken to insure that the sleeping hours would be as comfortable as possible. The room temperature was desirable, curtains were closed, warm blankets were provided and a night light was supplied.

4. Use of the bathroom at bedtime. This was encouraged to decrease the probability of "accidents."

Psychological: The following approach was used by the child care team in their contacts with Mike on a day-to-day basis. This was the most difficult part of the program to carry out and required a great deal of consistency, not only among Mike's three child care workers, but among all the adults who had contact with him.

1. A conscious effort was made on a daily basis to convey messages of support and encouragement to Mike. At any given time the adults asked themselves if his emotional needs were being met, and if not, what adjustments could be made. Anticipation of potential problem areas and extensive use of preventive planning were used to eliminate or reduce unnecessary anxiety-provoking situations. An attempt was made to incorporate this approach into every facet of Mike's day: school, group activities, casework, etc.

2. The child care worker on duty during the evening sought Mike out at bedtime for ten

or fifteen minutes of one-to-one interaction. The subject matter was usually initiated by Mike, with the child care worker continually reinforcing messages of support and interest. This evening contact was not contingent on his performance during the day. A similar one-to-one contact was made in the morning regardless of the condition of his bed.

3. Other staff members who were significant to Mike were made aware of the program and assisted in providing messages of support and encouragement. One staff member who had a positive relationship with Mike saw him twice a week on a scheduled basis for one-to-one involvement. This was time that Mike experienced success and enjoyment through high interest activities such as pool, woodworking and basketball.

Charting: Comprehensive records were kept for the sole purpose of assessing the effectiveness of the program. Mike was not aware of these charting procedures. (see Figure 10) This "consistency chart" was filled in by the child care worker on duty during the evening. After becoming familiar with the implementation of the program, the worker could predict with relative accuracy whether or not Mike's bed would be wet or dry the following morning. Using the chart also gave them great insight into what areas required their special attention, such as peer response or pertinent subject matter initiated by Mike at bedtime. Such

FIGURE 10   ENURESIS PROGRAM

Week of: 11/10–11/16   No.: 7

Item	Monday	Tuesday	Wednesday	Thursday	Friday	Saturday	Sunday
1. Elimination of fluids after 6:30 P.M.	Yes	Yes	Yes	Yes	Yes	Yes	Yes
2. Wearing pajamas at bedtime	Yes	Yes	Yes	Yes	Yes	Yes	Yes
3. Environmental adjustments (heat, curtains, blankets, light)	OK	OK	OK	OK	OK	OK	OK
4. Time spent with Mike at bedtime and subject matter initiated by Mike	Death Fear of dying	My future Marital life	Death Mother	Holidays Good times	Mother Foster homes	Radios	My apartment Beds Cats
5. Contacts with TH	OK	Woodworking	OK	Pool Woodworking	OK	OK	OK
6. Time with Mike on a 1:1 basis during the day	Basketball GO	In TV rm before bedtime MS	None	12 with JJ	10 minutes in TV room	None	None
7. Messages of support, encouragement and acceptance from worker	OK OK	OK OK	OK OK	OK OK	OK OK	OK OK	OK OK
8. Were Mike's emotional needs met during the day	Yes	Good day	Depressed at times	Yes	Yes. In good spirits	A rough day	No. Much less responsive to directions
9. Special observations of the day as related to Mike	Up and down	Relaxed at bedtime	Used bathroom 3 at bedtime	None	Good mood	Nervous	Argumentative
10. Response of peers to Mike	None	OK	OK	Same friction	Got along well	Conflict with JJ	None
11. Condition of bed following A.M. wet dry	Dry	Dry	Dry	Dry	Dry	Wet	Wet

information served as valuable warning signals to areas of conflict or unresolved anxiety.

Like the diet program , this program concentrated on many areas of growth. Several simpler programs had been tried previously, but this program was viewed as the impetus for elimination of the problem. The foundations for Mike's problem had to be dealt with throughout the day before he was ready to give up his bedwetting.

Summary

These child/youth workers were able to help Mike overcome his enuresis because they had the insight, skill and energy to develop a self-care program which included several effective intervention techniques and which focused attention on several interrelated facets of development. They recognized that there are no simple quick-fix solutions and thay had the fortitude to stick with their approach.

Two Mealtime Programs

Troubled youths often approach mealtime with unpleasant memories, mixed emotions and unusual eating habits. For example, they have often been underfed or overfed, had diets consisting of just sugar and starch, been deprived of food as punishment for unrelated behavior and learned to eat whenever they could get their hands on food. Consequently, child/youth workers must frequently develop programs to make mealtime a more meaningful or positive experience.

Following are two programs which were designed

to teach mealtime skills to two youths and to assure that the youths would have an opportunity to receive the nurturing and positive social interaction which are connected with a pleasant mealtime experience.

Jack

Jack was a boy who exhibited very primitive mealtime behavior. He was adept at putting the adult on the spot in the dining room. He would argue over the quantity of food others received, have temper tantrums and eat in the most obnoxious ways possible. This left the adult with the choice of either having to remove him from the room or ending up with a chaotic mealtime. Neither solution had a positive effect on Jack's or the group's eating habits.

Although Jack had a hearty appetite, he was constantly missing out on getting the food he needed. In analyzing the situation the team realized that food deprivation, whether self or externally imposed, had a very punitive effect on Jack. In other words, deprivation did nothing to help build relationships or develop better eating habits.

It was decided that a new approach was needed. The team also realized that this problem would not go away overnight. They wanted to do everything they could to help Jack have a decent meal, but they didn't want the rest of the group to have to suffer continually.

At a child care meeting it was noted that Jack responded to structure in other situations. This clue persuaded the team to try three techniques. First, Jack was told that if he chose to act out at dinner he would have to eat with another adult after the group was finished. Second, the team decided to serve Jack his food rather than allow him to grab for it. This set up the possibility that others would tease Jack, but the team felt they needed to control serving, at least until Jack began to show signs of improvement. The third technique was to gradually establish a beginning and an end to the meals. The workers would quietly remind Jack that dinner was about to begin and during the meal they would encourage him to concentrate on eating so that he'd be done in time for dessert.

These approaches provided some short and long term results. Since Jack had a strong desire to be part of the group he was reluctant to be removed. He also had a strong desire to be first and nothing was more intolerable than eating last. Jack was also relieved of the struggle to get the most food. Previously he ended up with quantities too overwhelming to eat. With the adult serving, he was faced with portions he could eat and assured that he could have more if he needed it. Jack also learned to pace himself, realizing it was better to eat with the group and have dessert at the same time they did than it was to goof around and have desert after the others finished.

Slowly Jack became more responsible at the table, and eventually he was able to serve himself. He began to enjoy many of the new foods he was trying, and he learned that there is self-satisfaction in being able to eat in the company of one's peers.

Mac

Mac was a twelve-year-old child who was being spoon fed up until the time he entered treatment. His parents viewed him as abnormal (minimal brain damage was indicated), and consequently treated him in a manner that fostered extreme dependence. This led to gross overeating and a complete lack of any ability on Mac's part to feed himself.

When Mac entered the center he refused to eat in front of others and he began to starve himself. As a precaution the agency doctor was consulted. He told the workers not to worry, that Mac would be able to sustain himself for awhile. He suggested Mac be offered the foods he found most enjoyable until he was ready to join the group at the meal table. In their search for the right program, the team had to be sensitive to the extreme anxiety Mac felt about eating meals in a new setting. Also, they realized that this anxiety was compounded by his lack of confidence in his ability to feed himself. Hence, the following step by step program was introduced:

1. Mac started by eating food of his own choosing, usually peanut butter, alone in his room.

2. One person, a child care worker, was introduced to eat with Mac. This was used as an instruction period and it gave Mac a chance to familiarize himself with a person who would be at the dinner table.

3. Mac was asked to clean himself and walk down to meals. He was also given the choice to eat or not eat at the table, with the option of coming back to his room to eat with an adult.

4. He was encouraged to eat at least part of his meal at the table. The remaining food could be taken back to his room.

5. Mac was asked to make eye contact and respond to others for part of his meal. The remainder of the meal was finished without interaction. This final procedure continued until Mac was eventually able to eat the whole meal at the table and interact with his peers throughout the mealtime.

The progression from one step to the next was dependent upon Mac's readiness to move on. The total program lasted approximately two months. For reinforcement Mac was given one new part of a five-piece magic kit each time he decided to try the next step. While on a specific step he was taught tricks that he could perform with his pieces from the magic kit. Each time he followed through with expections he was taught a new trick.

Two Grooming Programs

Grooming programs have an inherent advantage over most other programs in that the results are usually immediate and tangible. When youths are learning to comb their hair, wash their faces, wear clean or new clothes, make their beds or brush their teeth, they can usually see and enjoy the change while they are learning. Of course, some youths may not be ready for the positive change associated with good grooming, but most youths are surprised by the immediate pleasure they receive from completing grooming tasks which they ignored or were unable to complete in the past. Following are two brief examples of grooming programs which were designed for groups of troubled youths.

Sequential Grooming Tasks

This program was prepared to help a group of extremely dependent youths, ages approximately eight to eleven, learn to complete basic morning grooming routines. The workers began by identifying the series of sequential grooming tasks depicted in Figure 11 and by establishing individualized criteria for successful completion of these tasks on a daily basis. The tasks and the criteria were then discussed and agreed upon with the youths.

Next, each youth was given a copy of the grooming chart which was hung on the wall in the group TV room where all the youths could easily observe their point accumulations for task completion. Each point was worth one cent and a nickel was given on days when all the tasks were successfully completed. Points were cashed in at the end of the week.

Throughout the program the workers provided additional social reinforcement, praise and encouragement and they also provided instruction based on individual needs and abilities. A system was also devised to gradually remove the youths from the program. This system included a variable ratio reinforcement schedule and discussions about additional privileges and responsibilities that would ensue from being able to groom oneself.

This program was successful because this group of youth needed an easy to follow sequence of tasks, individualized instruction and support, and

FIGURE 11   SEQUENTIAL GROOMING PROGRAM

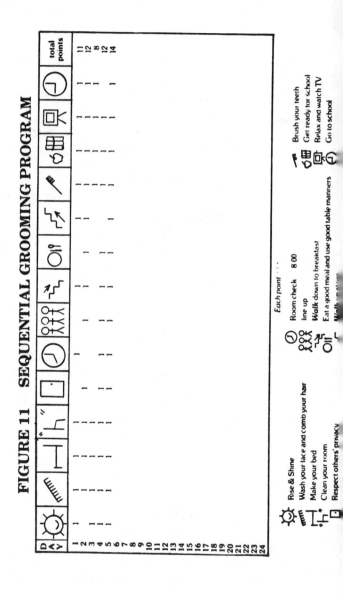

D A Y												total points
1	—	—	—	—	—	—	—	—	—	—	—	11
2	—	—	—	—	—	—	—	—	—	—	—	12
3	—	—	—	—	—	—	—	—	—	—	—	8
4	—	—	—	—	—	—	—	—	—	—	—	12
5	—	—	—	—	—	—	—	—	—	—	—	14
6												
7												
8												
9												
10												
11												
12												
13												
14												
15												
16												
17												
18												
19												
20												
21												
22												
23												
24												

Rise & Shine
Wash your face and comb your hair
Make your bed
Clean your room
Respect others' privacy

Each point ''s

Room check   8 00
line up
Walk down to breakfast
Eat a good meal and use good table manners
Walk up stairs

Brush your teeth
Get ready for school
Relax and watch TV
Go to school

a visual reminder of daily progress. Once the tasks were mastered most of the youths were able to continue because they gained self confidence and they found the tasks to be self satisfying.

Grooming Kits and Budgets

This program was prepared for a group of older, more independent boys who had a tendency to lose, destroy or misuse grooming articles such as deodorant, combs, brushes, soap and toothpaste. The youth had the basic skills to use and to take care of the articles, but for one reason or another they would usually opt not to use their skills, forcing the workers to hand out and collect each article every grooming period. The program objective, therefore, was to provide support and incentive for the youths to properly care for themselves and the arti les on their own.

The workers began by holding several discussions with the group to determine how the problem might be solved. During these discussions the workers pointed out how nice the youths looked when they used the articles and talked about how taking responsibility for their grooming articles was a first step in gaining more independence and responsibility in other areas. After much discussion the workers and the youths decided the articles should be earned one by one until all the articles were kept in the youths' bedrooms. If a youth lost or misused one article he would have to earn it back, but not lose the other articles he was using appropriately. Once all the articles were earned or being kept in the youth's room, he would receive a leather grooming kit and a monthly budget to purchase his choice of grooming articles to replace used articles.

The criteria for using and maintaining each article were individualized and throughout the program the workers provided individualized instruction and social reinforcement for task completion.

This type of program is effective with troubled youths who have basic grooming skills and who are capable of and desirous of additional independence and responsibility. Caution should always be taken to make sure that once youths receive the responsibility or privilege of having a kit and grooming budget that they will not fail or be unable to cope with the responsibility. But, in most cases, youths will respond if they have been involved in developing the program and the outcome is meaningful to their peers and them.

Medication Program

Troubled youths often take medications to help maintain their psychological and/or physical health. The example presented below was designed to help a youth assume more responsibility for taking medications.

Al

Al was taking medications to control seizures. The workers were routinely administering his pills to him, but Al showed little concern for taking the pills unless the adults took the initiative. To complicate matters, Al would play little games before he actually swallowed his pills. He would pretend to throw them away, spit them out, or hide them under his tongue. The workers wanted Al to show some initiative for taking his pills, and they wanted to be able to give him attention in more appropriate ways. They also realized that Al evidently did not feel he was worthy of being taken care of, and that it would take a concentrated effort before he could regularly show concern for himself.

The team decided to try to tie in taking medications with other daily self-caring functions. On Al's GAP chart (technique 3), the category "asking for medication" was included along with other basic categories. Each time Al did or did not ask for his medication, the team would mark the chart with a "yes" or "no." The child care workers would remind Al, at times other than the scheduled medication times, that it was important for him to ask for his medications. Al was told that if he did this frequently enough, along with his normal self-caring procedures, he could earn his own grooming kit, and eventually spend time alone in the music room before and after school. The adults also made a point of spending special time with Al on those days when he received a "yes."

This approach made it possible for Al to get the attention he needed in a more positive way, and it showed him that there were many advantages when he assumed responsibility for his own self-care. Most importantly, it showed Al that he was indeed worth taking care of.

Summary

The programs and techniques in this chapter were presented to show how child/youth workers integrate several intervention techniques into programs for addressing major self care areas. Readers should also have obtained an awareness of the understanding and intensity which is required to help youths develop basic self caring skills. Self-care takes many hours of work and growth can be slow, but the effort is worth it, especially when program success leads to growth in other areas of development.

1. Hudock, T. *Nocturnal enuresis in emotionally disturbed children: Treatment implications for the child care worker.* Paper submitted for publication.

CHAPTER SEVEN

SOCIAL INTERACTION PROGRAMS

The programs in this chapter were prepared by child/youth workers to help troubled youths assume more responsibility for daily social interactions with fellow group members and adults. Responsible social behavior has been defined as "the ability to fulfill one's needs and to do so in a way that does not deprive others of the right to fulfill their needs."[1] Troubled youths have difficulty being responsibile for three general reasons. First, they lack the self confidence and skill to meet their own needs. Second, they are often unaware of what their needs are, and finally, they often are unable to understand that others have needs of their own. These problems are further complicated by the fact that troubled youths in youth care programs generally interact with each other. Hence, child/youth workers must often prepare comprehensive programs to expose youths to the positive outcomes of responsible social behavior. This is not an easy task, but it is an essential task, because without an intensive effort to resolve these problems, the treatment environment can become extremely chaotic.

The following programs describe how focused attention can be placed on some common interaction problems and strengths. Readers will undoubtedly be able to identify several additional examples of their own. The task then is to explore how similar systematic approaches can be applied to situations in one's own environment and to recognize that programs are usually mutually interdependent with other facets of treatment plans. For example, the reader will note that there is some intentional overlapping with the last chapter, because self-care and social interaction are usually mutually dependent.

The programs chosen for this chapter are titled:

1. The Scapegoat
2. The Parent
3. The Hitter
4. The Tough Guy
5. Level System One
6. Level System Two

Four Individual Programs

The first four programs, "the scapegoat," "the parent," "the hitter," and "the tough guy" are individual programs for youths who have specific social behavior problems. Most troubled youths have certain behavior patterns that interfere more than others with their ability to interact with others.

1. "The Scapegoat"

Jan's initial treatment plan indicated he was a youth who was easily scapegoated. Early intervention techniques were used to discourage the other boys' attempts to set Jan up as a scapegoat, and to make Jan more self-aware through individual therapy and self-caring programs. At this point in treatment, Jan was capable of receiving positive feedback from his peers, but he still allowed himself to be placed in the uncomfortable position of group scapegoat. He would turn into the group clown, defy adults or tease another youth at the slightest prompting from his peers. The workers felt Jan must have been receiving a certain amount of gratification from the negative attention he was receiving or he would have been more willing to give up this behavior. It was also possible that Jan did not think he could meet his needs, as he perceived them, in any other way. The following techniques were used to show Jan he could meet his needs without inconveniencing or being rejected by others.

1. Charts and log notes indicated that Jan interacted most productively when structure was provided. Consequently, staff members concentrated on planning Jan's day so that his strengths, rather than his weaknesses, could be emphasized. For example, group activities that capitalized on Jan's coordination and stamina were regularly included in the day's events. He was also complimented in front of the group for his appearance, which was usually very neat. This type of planned intervention opened many avenues for easy travel to the "in-group," rather than having Jan constantly occupy the spot of "isolate."

2. Jan could behave very well if other youths weren't around or insisting on him being the scapegoat. Thus, an attempt was made to encourage him to use his ability to function independently to his own advantage. He enjoyed building puzzles in his room and was capable of engaging in constructive conversation with boys who were behaving

responsibly. Two periods were chosen for Jan to use these strengths independently of adult supervision. Whether or not he got to use these periods was contingent on how well he avoided being scapegoated during stressful periods. The first period was in the morning before school. If Jan was able to perform all his morning routines before school started he could have up to 30 minutes to work on puzzles. New puzzles were provided as needed. The second period was in the evening before bedtime. If Jan completed his showering and room cleaning tasks, he could spend the remainder of his time in the recreation room with other responsible youths. Of course, if Jan chose, as he had in the past, to be group scapegoat during either period he would not be left unsupervised. The worker's role was to remind Jan that he had two alternatives to choose from. Although the final choice was his, the adults stressed the advantages of responsible behavior. Since the self caring tasks themselves were easy for Jan to perform, it did not take him long to regularly choose the positive alternative.

3. Jan obviously identified with the role of scapegoat or he wouldn't continue to fill it. In an attempt to help him identify with a more appropriate image, a significant male child/youth care worker and Jan's therapist were asked to seek Jan out for one-to-one involvement. They would seek Jan out when he was behaving responsibly and ask him to

shoot some baskets, go for a walk or help him with a special project. This accomplished two goals. It helped show Jan that he had the ability to behave like males he admired and it helped solidify his relationship with two very important people.

4. Part of Jan's willingness to be scapegoated was seen as an opportunity to indirectly express his anger. In his clowning around, he would break things and his teasing sometimes led to hitting and fighting. The things he broke or people he hurt were usually not directly responsible for his behavior. Therefore, whenever the opportunity arose, the workers would encourage him to express his angry feelings toward the correct person. They assured him that no harm would come to him for being honest. Praise was given each time the workers felt Jan was being direct. The workers kept track of this on a weekly basis and discussed the results with Jan. If he had made a good attempt to be honest and direct he was taken off grounds by one of the two persons mentioned previously. Once again it did not take long before Jan began to choose the more responsible way of interacting.

2. "The Parent"

Lee had two major behavior problems that kept him from being an accepted part of the group. The first problem resulted from a lack of strong male models in Lee's family life. He grew up in a family where he was forced to play father to his siblings at a very young age. This proved to be a disastrous experience for Lee and his family. When Lee tried to transfer his inept parenting skills to the treatment center he was immediately rejected. Lee was constantly telling others what to do, minding their business or tattling to the workers. Needless to say, the group members found this to be a totally unacceptable way of interacting. Even though Lee had several positive characteristics, he seldom got a chance to exhibit them. His peers would isolate him or refuse to give him any positive support during their activities.

Lee's second behavior problem centered around his interactions with adults, but it also fed into further rejection from the group. Lee felt he could only please adults by giving them things or by doing things for them. He would not accept praise or encouragement for efforts toward his own development. Instead, he would awkwardly offer the adults presents, or ask them to be a helper at precisely the wrong time. It was almost as if he sensed that the adults would be too busy or occupied with someone else to respond the way he wanted them to. Consequently, the adults would get angry with Lee for his constant pestering and other group members saw his behavior as an attempt to be the worker's pet. Neither situation did much to help Lee meet his real needs and it certainly was viewed as an interference by others. The following techniques were used to help Lee interact more responsibly:

1. Again, group activities were planned that accentuated Lee's strengths. In Lee's case,

these were table games, woodworking or arts and crafts projects. The workers encouraged Lee to relax and enjoy himself while assuring him that they would assume responsibility for the other boys' behavior. Lee was also told that if he successfully completed activities without bossing or tattling on others he could work on a special project during free time and before bedtime. Both periods immediately followed group activities. The projects — car models, paint by numbers, or building with an erector set — were things that Lee did well and enjoyed. These projects required several periods to complete. This created an ongoing incentive for Lee to interact appropriately throughout the day. Once a project was finished, the adults encouraged Lee to keep it and display it for others to see. Instead of permitting him to give it away, they would spend special time with Lee building a display case or shelves to put his projects on.

2. Special efforts were made to talk with Lee on an individual basis. This was usually done before bed when Lee had just finished working on a project. The adults would stress the advantages of being a youth and assure him that it was okay for him to act like the other youths. They also tried to relieve him of the burden of having to feel as if he needed to take control of others' lives. Without criticizing his family, the adults very delicately tried to let Lee know that it was their job to run the group. They asked Lee to concentrate on meeting his

own needs. For example, Lee was doing very well on his own self-care and he received a great deal of pleasure from looking nice. The adults tried to point out how similar attempts to concentrate on his own efforts could also be self-satisfying within the group. He was assured that the other boys were more likely to respond positively to the things he did well than they would to his attempts to control or parent them.

3. "The Hitter"

Greg had a great deal of difficulty directly expressing his angry feelings. Several factors contributed to his inability to tell others when he was mad. To begin with, his speech development was very slow. He had trouble finding the right words and he lacked enough confidence in his speaking to be able to tell others when or why he was angry. Greg's perception of his ability to stand up to others was also very limited. Although he was as big, if not bigger, than the other boys, he felt he was defenseless against them. Thus, when Greg was angry at one of the boys, he would strike out at the nearest adult who he knew would not retaliate. This created a very tenuous situation for the workers, who were not always able to predict when Greg was mad. He could strike out at any moment without their being aware of what was going on. Several attempts had been made to discuss Greg's angry feelings with him, but he was unable to process most of what the adults were saying. The adults also felt uncomfortable with this approach because Greg would tend to take their interpretations as fact, rather than as possibilities. In other words, they could be wrong about why Greg was feeling angry, but he would take their interpretations literally as the reason why he was angry and become even more confused. It was decided that a simpler, more concrete approach was needed. The following techniques were chosen:

1. A reward system was established to give Greg a piece of candy for each thirty-minute time period in which he did not hit, push or kick at an adult. In school Greg was given an additional reward of spending special time with the teacher or teaching assistant for each day that he did not hit at all. Greg was also praised and encouraged for legitimate expressions of anger. It was sufficient for him simply to say he was mad at someone, but the workers also encouraged him to try to explain why. If he could not, no additional pressure was placed on him.

2. An alternative object at which to direct his anger was provided for Greg. If he felt the need to strike out, he was permitted to go to the exercise room and punch the heavy bag. Greg was praised and encouraged for making this choice the same as if he had made a verbal expression of his anger. On the other hand, if Greg made an attempt to hit the adult, he was removed to his room until he was able to express himself more appropriately. These first two steps quickly reduced the amount of hitting Greg did. This freed the adults to

concentrate on the next step . . .

3. Projects were designed to help Greg establish a
    more realistic perception of himself. During
    one group activity, for example, the children
    traced each other's bodies on large sheets of
    paper. The finished projects were then hung
    together on the living room wall. Group
    pictures were also taken and placed in a frame
    on the recreation room wall. Projects like this
    gave Greg a better idea of how his physical size
    compared with the rest of the boys in the group.

Other techniques were used to point out that many
of Greg's abilities were as good, if not better than
some of the other boys. Greg was good at drawing
pictures, and he had good gross motor
coordination. Activities that emphasized these
strengths showed Greg that he was not totally
defenseless. Even though his communication
skills were limited, there were many other things
he could do quite well. Gradually, Greg began to
feel more comfortable in group interactions,
realizing that there was no real reason for him to
feel intimidated. His peers began to respect him for
his strengths and they reduced their attempts to
make him angry.

4. **"The Tough Guy"**

Gary was a youth who had a hard time
separating the real world from his fantasy world.
In his interactions with others, he would take on
the role of his favorite television heroes.
Unfortunately, these heroes were usually quite
violent characters. The hard-nosed cop or the

private detective, skilled in martial arts, were the people he chose to imitate. Gary would push his weight around, constantly have his hands on others and talk in a threatening manner. The workers realized that this was all a cover-up for his real feelings of inadequacy, but it was difficult to talk with Gary when he was threatening to "blow their heads off," "kick their butts in" or "throw them in the slammer." When the workers were able to get through to Gary, he would take a very defensive posture and, like his heroes, convey the impression that he could do no wrong. Gary's peers were very irritated with his behavior, but most of them were too intimidated to say anything to him.

Underneath it all, Gary was a very insecure and frightened youth. He was extremely dependent on the adults and the treatment center. For example, he could be trusted to go off grounds alone, but he seldom was willing to leave the secure surroundings of the center. When asked to go off grounds, he would come up with some excuse, such as "What do I want to go there for, I do that when I'm on my home visit," or "That's kid stuff." The truth of the matter was that Gary spent most of his home visits in the house watching television and wishing that he could have more child-like experiences. As a result of his behavior, Gary had a very limited knowledge of the real world and he continually missed out on age-appropriate group and community experiences. The workers decided to take an approach that would assure Gary that they liked him for who he was and that would show him that he could receive more satisfaction from interacting age-appropriately.

1. All the adults agreed that they became very irritated when Gary placed his hands on them or threatened them. They decided that alternatives would have to be found if they were going to be able to positively approach Gary. A handshake seemed like the most reasonable substitute for the hand-placing situation. This put the adults somewhat in control, but it did not deprive Gary of his need to have physical contact with others. It also was a much more appropriate way of interacting. At first the workers found themselves shaking hands with Gary several times a day. He would also squeeze their hand and hold it for a period of time, but both parties found this to be a more comfortable situation. Eventually, Gary reduced his touching and handshaking considerably. He realized that he could get the contact he needed without rejecting others in the process.

Dealing with the threats was a somewhat more difficult process. Threatening remarks usually were a good indication of when Gary was feeling very anxious and inadequate. If adults responded negatively or tried to correct Gary, he became even more defensive and threatening. Ignoring did not work because Gary was usually intent on getting the adult's attention one way or another. If they were not available his peers would suffer the consequences. The workers decided that they would have to be patient with this problem while taking a positive reassuring approach. When Gary was using threats, the workers tried to calmly assure him that they were interested in helping him with what was really bothering him. They would tell him that this could be done more easily if they could talk to the real Gary and not to one of his heroes. Their message was that Gary really could handle his problems and that he didn't have to pretend to be someone else. This approach took a great deal of perseverance and some cheek turning on the part of the workers, but Gary did eventually realize that his anxiety could be relieved more easily by being himself.

2. The second part of the program was designed to put Gary in touch with the real world outside the treatment center. The workers wanted to show Gary that he could interact in the community, but first they needed to show him that living in the world does not have to be a violent, threatening experience. Special activities were designed to place Gary in day-to-day community situations that he could learn to deal with if he used his own strengths. Bus rides, using the laundromat, pricing articles at the store, buying the food for a meal, going to a local block party, and picking up the newspaper at the drug store were just a few of the community experiences Gary was exposed to. In each case, Gary was accompanied by an adult until he felt comfortable going on his own. Gary began to realize that others — the

storekeeper, the checkout girl, or the policeman on the corner — responded much better when he acted like himself and not some tough guy. Gary did have very appealing looks and a pleasant tone of voice. On the unit, the workers would remind Gary that when he approached others with a smile, polite words or an honest expression of feelings, they in turn would generally respond supportively. Gradually, Gary began to gain the self-confidence he needed to interact with others. He also found that it was much more satisfying to express his feelings appropriately and that the adults could help him with his anxiety if they did not have to first deal with the tough guy.

Level Programs

Level programs are group programs which are usually based on some form of privilege system (see 18. Privilege Systems). In other words, the workers and the youths sit down together and discuss the relationship between responsible social behavior and the privileges that result from that behavior. The program then serves as constant encouragement and support for group members to work toward productive social interaction. The two programs in this section represent two different approaches to developing a level program.

Level System One

The need for this system was brought to the worker's attention through the recurrence of one specific theme during group discussions. The youths were regularly reverting to the issue of fairness. They were eager to know why one youth could be trusted to have certain privileges and another could not. The workers would try to answer these questions by explaining that trust developed in relationships when both parties were willing to assume responsibility for their interactions. They assured the youths that each youth would eventually obtain privileges, but it would take time before they all would get to know each other well enough to be able to interact responsibly on a regular basis. Unfortunately, this line of reasoning didn't get through to the youths. This was a younger, dependent group that had difficulty comprehending discussions of this nature. No matter how hard the workers tried, the youths still viewed privileges as something the adults gave to those they favored. They could not see the connection between their own behavior and their ability to obtain privileges. To them, trusted youths were the ones the adults liked the best.

Obviously, something more concrete had to be done to get the group on the right track. Up to this point, the workers thought they had been effectively using privileges on an individual basis, but an examination of the plans indicated just the opposite. Only one youth was permitted to have privileges that encouraged some degree of independence, and even he wasn't doing very well. The other youths had not been consistently following through with their responsibilities, but they were capable of more than they were showing. One difficulty lay in the fact that privileges were only related to self-caring programs and not to the youths' ability to interact with each other. The second problem was that since the members hadn't experienced success with privileges they really didn't know what it felt like to have privileges. This lack of understanding and the fear of losing the attention they had been receiving, regardless of whether it had been positive or negative, really did little to discourage their irresponsibile behavior. The workers decided to implement the following program:

1. Several weekly meetings were used to discuss the types of behavior that could help rather than interfere with others' rights to meet their own needs. Since the group in general lacked a great deal of insight, and had little perception of how others felt, the behavior discussed was simplistic and well within the capabilities of each group member. Following is a list of some of these behavior patterns:

   1. Get up in the morning without disturbing others.

   2. Listen to the workers during group activities.

   3. Take care of the group games.

   4. Tell others when you are angry, don't hit or swear at them.

   5. Tell others when you are sad or afraid, don't run away or refuse to play with the group.

   6. Share the group toys, don't hog them for yourself.

(Much more behavior was discussed, but this brief list gives the reader an idea of the level on which these youths were functioning.)

2. At the next series of meetings the workers listed the privileges they felt were most appropriate and the group discussed how they could be obtained. (It was understood that new boys would be supervised at all times.)

    1. Can visit with another boy in his room or in an activity area without adult supervision. (This could be done primarily during rest periods.)

    2. Can go outside alone to play with other unsupervised youth. (This can be done on grounds only.)

    3. Can go off grounds to the store.

    4. Can be involved in a community activity, such as YMCA, swimming lessons, the Boy's Club, etc., and go alone into the community for special events.

    The youths asked that they be able to request to be moved from one level to the next when they felt they were ready. Each week the adults would consider their requests and discuss whether the youths had been consistently performing the behavior they had discussed at the meetings. This included following through with their self-caring programs. The workers also helped the youths understand that they couldn't expect to move from one level to the next without successfully experiencing their privileges on one level for a reasonable period of time. This approach opened several avenues for growth. First of all, the adults had an opportunity to discuss each youth's behavior individually on a regular basis. Even if the youth's request was denied, the workers could sit down with the youth and tell him why. They could also reassure him that he had the ability to move up eventually and, when a youth succeeded, the workers could point out how his own behavior was responsible for his movement. Another advantage was the behavior a youth developed while experiencing that a privilege on one level was helpful on the next. For example, if a youth could get along with a friend in his room (level one), he had a better chance of succeeding in level two where he would be able to play with youths from other groups outdoors.

Of course, if a youth failed to respond appropriately, or abused his privileges once he had obtained a certain level, the adults couldn't permit him to be unsupervised. The group decided that if this happened, a youth should temporarily be restricted from his privileges. The workers went to great lengths to make certain this didn't happen too frequently. Individual programs were designed for those youths who had problems with a specific behavior, and the workers constantly encouraged all the youths to maintain their level of performance. The workers didn't want privileges to be seen as something adults gave or took away each time a youth was good or bad.

Level System Two

In the previous program, adults played a very active role in setting up the level system. The following program is an example of how a level system can be designed with more input from the youths. This system was used with an older, more mature group of youths who had been functioning with some degree of independence prior to the program.

1. The group began by prioritizing privileges. The order went as follows:

   a. Having one's own grooming materials.

   b. Watching TV with others during leisure time.

   c. Visiting others during rest periods.

   d. 9:30 bedtime — this included staying up with other boys watching TV or playing table games.

   e. 10:00 o'clock bedtime.

   f. Doing routines without adult supervision.

   g. Work for pay — first on grounds and then in the community.

   h. Off grounds without supervision — this included community activities, special events and just going for a walk.

2. The youths divided the day into crucial time periods that they felt required maximum group

cooperation. These periods included all the times when the group was either performing routines or participating in group activities. They discussed all the behavior they felt would interfere with the rights of one or more members of the group to be productive participants. During these discussions the adults steered the conversation away from extremes, and they discouraged the youths from becoming personal in their descriptions of behavior.

Once the irresponsible behavior was clearly defined, the youths asked the adults to monitor the system for them. They wanted the adults to give them a point for each period they were responsible and then, on a daily or weekly basis cash these points in for privileges. The adults suggested that, rather than have an across the board point system, obtaining a certain privilege could perhaps be based on how well a youth handled those periods that correlated with times when the privileges would be or had been used. Many of the group members had obtained "grooming kits," "visiting" or "later bedtime" privileges on an individual basis. The workers pointed out that they were able to have these privileges because they had shown the ability to use grooming kits and visit or stay up without disrupting others. Other privileges, such as "off grounds," "work for pay" or doing routines," could be handled in the same way except that these privileges would require responsible behavior in many areas. The youth who went off grounds would have to be responsible throughout the day, or the workers would have no indication that he would be able to handle similar experiences in the community. Working for pay would require that the youth be able to handle daily routines, as well as cooperate with others during activities and projects, or there would be no indication that they could work and cooperate with less familiar persons. The youths concurred with the workers' suggestions and asked that they be able to request a privilege when they felt they were ready. This gave the workers the same opportunity for individual discussions that the previous example provided.

This group was able to discuss responsible behavior and capable of relating their behavior to privileges. Therefore, in this system, the adults' role was to facilitate discussion, to monitor progress and to individualize the system so that one youth or another was not constantly missing out on acquiring privileges. This type of situation is very conducive to developing responsible social interactions within groups of troubled youth.

Summary

The programs in this and the previous chapter epitomize what child/youth workers can do when they work together to systematically address major areas of growth and development. These programs were presented with the hope that readers will be inspired by the workers' creativity and tenacity to develop similar approaches at their agencies. Child/youth care is no longer viewed as a job which can be mastered with common sense and spontaneous reactions. It is a craft or science which is based on teamwork, advance planning and systematic intervention.

1. Glasser, W. *Reality therapy.*New York: Harper and Row, 1965.

BIBLIOGRAPHY AND
SUGGESTED READINGS

Ainsworth, F., & Fulcher, L. (Eds.) *Group care for children.*New York: Tavistock Publications, 1981.

Beker, J. The emergence of clinical youthwork as a profession: Implications for the youthwork field. *Center for Youth Development and Research Quarterly Focus*, University of Minnesota, 1980.

Beker, J., Gittelson, P., Husted, S., Kaminstein, P., & Finkler Adler, L. *Critical incidents in child care: A case study book.* New York: Behavioral Publications, 1972.

Bergin, A., & Garfield, S. *Handbook of psychotherapy and behavior change.*New York: John Wiley and Sons, 1971.

Bettlheim, B. *Love is not enough.* Glencoe, Illinois: Free Press, 1950.

Conger, J. *Adolescence and youth: Psychological development in a changing world.* New York: Harper and Row, 1979.

Driekurs, R. & Cassels, P. *Discipline without tears.* New York: Hawthorne Books, 1974.

Dreikurs, R., & Gray, L. *Logical consequences,* New York: Hawthorne Books, 1969.

Foster, G., VanderVen, K., Kroner, E., Carbonara, N., & Cohen, G. *Child care work with emotionally disturbed children.* Pittsburgh: University of Pittsburgh Press, 1972.

Garner, H. *Teamwork in programs for children and youth.* Springfield, Illinois: Charles C. Thomas Publisher, 1982.

Ginot, H. *Between parent and child.* New York: McMillan, 1965.

Glasser, W. *Reality therapy.* New York: Harper and Row, 1965.

Gordon, T. *Parent workbook.* Pasadena, California: Effectiveness Training Association, 1972.

Krueger, M. Child care worker involvement in research, *Journal of Child Care,* 18a, 1982, *1,* (1).

Krueger, M. The effectiveness of a dieting program on emotionally disturbed children. *Child Welfare League of America,* 1973, vol. LII.

Krueger, M. *Implementation of a team decision-making model among child care workers.* Doctoral Dissertation, University of Wisconsin — Milwaukee, 1982.

Krueger, M. *Job satisfaction for child care workers.* Milwaukee, Wisconsin: Tall Publishing, 1981.

Krueger, M. & Nardine, F. The Wisconsin child care worker survey. (Forthcoming in the *Child Care Quarterly*).

Lerner, R. *Concepts and theories of human development.* Reading Mass: Addison Wesely, 1976.

Maier, H. The core of care: Essential ingredients for the development of children away from home. *Child Care Quarterly,* 1979, *8,* (3), 161-173.

Mayer, J. *A guide for child care workers.* New York: Child Welfare League of America, 1958.

Meyer, J. An exploratory nationwide survey of child care workers. *Child Care Quarterly*, 1980, *9*, (1).

Porter, C. VanderVen, K. & Mattingly, M. *Perspectives on educating for child and youth care practice. Outcomes of the initial Conference — Research Sequence in Child Care Education,* University of Pittsburg, 1980.

Redl, F., & Wineman, D. *The aggressive child.* Glencoe, Illinois: The Free Press, 1957.

Savicki, V., & Brown, R. *Working with troubled children.* New York: Human Sciences Press, 1981.

Trieschman, A., Wittaker, J., & Brendtro, L. *The other twenty three hours.* Chicago, Illinois: Aldine, 1969.

VanderVen, K. Towards maximum effectiveness of the unit team approach in residential care: An agenda for team development. *Residential and Community Child Care Administration, 1*, (3), 1979, 287-297.

VanderVen, K., Mattingly, M., & Morris, M.Principles and guidelines for child care personnel preparation programs. *Child Care Quarterly*, 1982, *11*, (3).

Whitaker, J. *Caring for troubled children.* San Francisco, California: Jossey Bass, 1980.

Wilson, T., Powell, N. & Winer, T. The Maryland Association of Child Care Workers Survey, 1976.